SY 0126147 9

The Essenti   Dickens
School Resc

Charles Dickens is arguably the greatest storyteller in English literature and his novels have been loved and respected for nearly two hundred years. As accurate reflections of Victorian society they are unparalleled. Vivid characters and realistic settings are created in the mind of the reader, all laced with Dickens' inimitable humour, wit and lacerating political comment.

This book aims to bring alive these characters and settings in the minds of children. It provides a comprehensive resource not only for children to learn about the literary heritage of the English language, but also to encourage them to create meanings from these classic stories through their personal, social and cultural experiences. The authors set each novel in context, providing a synopsis of the book, as well as characters, settings, themes and symbolism. The works covered are:

- *A Christmas Carol*
- *Bleak House*
- *David Copperfield*
- *Great Expectations*
- *Hard Times*
- *Oliver Twist*

But this book doesn't just aim to introduce classic literature to children; it also provides a wide range of truly contemporary tools with which they can respond creatively, including drama and film, blogs, Web 2.0 technologies, multimodality and animation, and graphic novels.

The book is also accompanied by a CD that contains chapter outlines, extended text extracts and practical resource sheets, including PowerPoint presentations, book review templates and flash cards, as well as a set of 8-week lesson plans for each novel.

The Essential Charles Dickens School Resource provides essential classroom learning material for teachers and literacy coordinators teaching Key Stages 1–3, as well as CPD students and those studying on PGCE English/drama courses.

Gill Robins is the former deputy head teacher of Sun Hill Junior School in Hampshire. She received the UKLA John Downing Award in 2010. Until 2011 she chaired the English Association Editorial Board for the *English 4–11* journal.

Laura-Jane Evans-Jones is a recently qualified English teacher who also sat on the TES English Teaching panel from 2010 to 2011.

The Essential Charles Dickens School Resource

Contemporary approaches to teaching classic texts ages 7–14

Gill Robins and
Laura-Jane Evans-Jones

Routledge
Taylor & Francis Group

LONDON AND NEW YORK

First published 2012
by Routledge
2 Park Square, Milton Park, Abingdon, Oxon OX14 4RN

Simultaneously published in the USA and Canada
by Routledge
711 Third Avenue, New York, NY 10017

Routledge is an imprint of the Taylor & Francis Group, an informa business

© 2012 Gill Robins and Laura-Jane Evans-Jones

The right of Gill Robins and Laura-Jane Evans-Jones to be identified as authors of this work has been asserted by them in accordance with sections 77 and 78 of the Copyright, Designs and Patents Act 1988.

All rights reserved. No part of this book may be reprinted or reproduced or utilised in any form or by any electronic, mechanical, or other means, now known or hereafter invented, including photocopying and recording, or in any information storage or retrieval system, without permission in writing from the publishers.

Trademark notice: Product or corporate names may be trademarks or registered trademarks, and are used only for identification and explanation without intent to infringe.

British Library Cataloguing in Publication Data
A catalogue record for this book is available from the British Library

Library of Congress Cataloging in Publication Data
Robins, Gill.
The essential Charles Dickens school resource: contemporary approaches to teaching classic texts ages 7-14 / Gill Robins, Laura-Jane Evans-Jones.
p. cm.
1. Dickens, Charles, 1812-1870—Study and teaching. 2. Dickens, Charles, 1812-1870—Sources. 3. Dickens, Charles, 1812-1870—Criticism and interpretation. I. Evans-Jones, Laura-Jane. II. Title.
PR4588.R57 2012
823'.8—dc23
2011039486

ISBN: 978-0-415-69555-8 (pbk)
ISBN: 978-0-203-14485-5 (ebk)

Typeset in Helvetica
by FiSH Books, Enfield

MIX
Paper from
responsible sources
FSC® C004839
www.fsc.org

Printed and bound in Great Britain by the MPG Books Group

Contents

CD
A Christmas Carol
Bleak House
David Copperfield
Great Expectations
Hard Times
Oliver Twist

Acknowledgements

We would like to thank the Royal Shakespeare Company for their permission to use the Whoosh drama activity.

Thank you to Gingy Jack, John Robins and Andrew Scott for IT support and to Nafeesa Ahmed for her encouragement.

Many thanks to Jim Evans-Jones and John Robins for their support and enthusiasm throughout the writing of this book.

Preface

2012 is the bicentenary of the birth of Charles Dickens, arguably England's finest storyteller. His novels reflect a significant chapter in English social history – the mass migration of workers from land to city during the Industrial Revolution, with all the attendant problems of unemployment, overcrowding, homelessness and deprivation. Dickens brings the poverty and privilege of Victorian England into sharp focus, particularly as it related to children.

But another reason why Dickens' books remain so popular is our love of storytelling. It is through storying that we all make sense of our lives and relate issues to our experience at many levels, whether this is recounting an incident of the day to a friend, using a social networking site, writing a story or making a film. Media stories about celebrity life feed an insatiable public curiosity: at a personal level, millions of stories are narrated and blogged daily on Facebook, MSN and Twitter. Google declares one site to be 'an open, engaging, and fun environment that empowers a new generation to discover, connect and express themselves' – an opportunity for digital storytelling on a global scale.

It is important that children learn about the literary heritage of the English language and Dickens' two-hundredth birthday seems an ideal opportunity for a lavish celebration. However, it is also equally important that children are able to make meaning from these classic stories through their personal, social and cultural experiences. So, as far as possible, activities relate the Victorian world of Dickens' characters to the twenty-first-century world of the modern child. Response media are also contemporary, so suggested activities might include film, animation, Web 2.0 technologies or graphic novelling. But whatever the medium for response, the character types remain universal, as are the themes of loss, dishonesty, exploitation, bullying, friendship, loyalty and the power of good to triumph over evil. Ben Jonson's view of Shakespeare in 1623, 'He is not of an age, but for all time,' could equally apply to Charles Dickens.

The book opens with a chapter containing detailed explanations of some contemporary approaches which can be used in teaching classic texts. Each chapter starts by setting the novel in context, followed by a synopsis of the book, major and minor character lists, settings and the symbolism of the novel. If you are working with young children, you can use just the major characters and the main plot, or you can weave in sub plots and less important characters when working with older children. This is followed by a range of activities which are aimed at helping children to relate the characters, their lives, actions and reactions to themselves and their own experiences. To help to develop this understanding, each chapter ends with suggestions for linked reading, both fiction and non-fiction. A resource section at the end of the book contains suggestions for helpful websites, a Dickens booklist which is broadly age differentiated and a general interest booklist.

You might choose to pursue one theme such as poverty, hunger or child labour, or compare and contrast two characters such as Oliver Twist and David Copperfield. However you choose to introduce your children to Dickens, you can find ideas to help you. It is important that some use is made of Dickens' own language – Marcia Williams' book *Oliver Twist and Other Great Dickens Stories* is a good example of how even very young children can be introduced to this. Although captions are used to narrate the story, the characters in the pictures use the actual language of the characters in the books. Explore ways of creating multimodal texts which use original language. Older children could explore ways of 'translating' examples of the original text into modern English in the way that the Classic Comics graphic novels do or they could produce manga texts.

The way the stories are introduced is important – for young children you could use the Usborne Young Readers CDs to listen to the story. You might read the story in instalments, in the same spirit in which many of the stories were written. Alternatively you could provide good quality picture books, learn the story and tell it yourself or use a professional storyteller, which would make the experience very special. Whichever resources you choose, it is important to familiarise young children with the story before starting to study it. For older children, use chosen sections of the full text or the Classic Comics graphic novels. Ensure that your chosen theme, character or sections of text are really familiar both to yourself and the children before you start any response activities – there are plenty of suggestions to support familiarisation with the text in the following chapters.

For clear organisation, the activities are grouped together by title and under the headings of *Hooks, starters and pause points*, *Understanding character*, *Understanding plot*, *Understanding setting* and *Whole text responses*, but there is no reason why, with some adaptation, they could not relate across the titles. And whilst some activities are clearly suitable for a particular age group, others can be adapted for use across the age range. Suggested ages for each activity are marked with one star (*) for 7 to 9-year-olds, two stars (**) for 9 to 11-year-olds and three stars (***) for 11 to 14-year-olds, although these are intended only as guidelines. We hope that this book reaches as wide an audience as possible in the cause of celebration, whether you are part of a small group, one class, a whole school or a cluster of schools.

The book is accompanied by a CD which contains relevant text extracts, resource sheets, chapter outlines, figurative language examples and planning suggestions. For younger pupils, the planning is themed, with some themes such as *School days* and *Houses and homes* linked across two or more titles. For older pupils, planning is titled *Whole text plan 11–14* and each scheme of work suggests a different outcome, from an extended blogging project in *Great Expectations* to a media studies unit for *Bleak House*. You may want to explore just one aspect of a book, or you may want to use the suggested activities in the book to build your own plan.

We hope that you enjoy using this book as much as we have enjoyed writing it. All the activities arise from our own classroom practice so they are tried and tested, but it is your enthusiasm for sharing the stories which will lift the characters off of the page and bring them to life for your pupils.

Gill Robins
Laura-Jane Evans-Jones
August 2011

Biography of Charles Dickens

Charles John Huffam Dickens, the second of John and Elizabeth Dickens' seven children, was born on 7 February 1812 in Portsmouth – the house in which he was born is now a museum. In 1814 his family moved to London, living a few houses away from the Cleveland Street workhouse. Then, two years later, the family moved to Chatham, where his father worked as a Navy Pay Clerk. In 1822, facing financial problems, the family returned to London. One account relates how Charles, as a child, would recite ballads and tell stories for the clerks in his father's office. He was an avid reader – David Copperfield's devouring of the books which he discovered reflects Dickens' own childhood love of reading.

Charles was educated privately until his father, whose generosity had led to him spending well beyond the family's modest income, was sent to Marshalsea Debtors Prison, which was later used as a setting in *Little Dorrit.* The rest of his family was also sent to live in the prison, but Charles lodged locally and at the age of just twelve, was forced to leave school and work pasting labels on black shoe polish in a warehouse. He earned very little money, the work was hard and he was surrounded by grinding poverty – an experience which shaped his future narrative both in settings and the characters whom he met. His family's ruin was reversed when a relative died, leaving enough money to pay off the debt. Charles was not immediately recalled from the warehouse although he was eventually able to complete his education at Wellington House Academy, a school which became fictionalised in *David Copperfield*, a character who is presumed to be broadly autobiographical.

After leaving school at fifteen to work in a solicitor's office, he decided that he wanted to pursue a career in journalism. Through court reporting, he acquired the perceptive view of the law immortalised in *Bleak House.* His ambition, however, was to become a parliamentary reporter, which he achieved at the age of just nineteen. He reported for the *True Sun*, the *Mirror of Parliament* and finally the *Morning Chronicle*. Following publication of his *Sketches by Boz* and his first novel, *Pickwick Papers*, in 1836, Dickens established himself as an author. Throughout his life, he edited magazines and journals, lectured widely against social injustice and conducted more than four hundred readings of his own novels, many of which were written and published in instalments.

He married Catherine Hogarth, also in 1836, and they had ten children. He died at the age of 58 after suffering a stroke and despite his wish to be buried in Rochester Cathedral, Kent, where he lived, he was buried in Poets' Corner in Westminster Abbey. His tombstone reads, 'He was a sympathiser to the poor, the suffering, and the oppressed; and by his death, one of England's greatest writers is lost to the world.'

1 Contemporary approaches

Multimodality

We communicate through a range of modes, known as semiotic systems. There are five modes:

- *Gesture* can be organised into intentional movement as in dance, mime or acting. We also communicate spontaneously with body language – a more powerful mode than spoken language. Where body and spoken language conflict, body language predominates.
- *Sound* includes music and sound effects (which are chosen to achieve a particular effect) and the tone of spoken language, which can be consciously controlled to convey meaning or can unintentionally betray a subtext or subconscious feeling.
- *Vision* encompasses all that we see and is used as a communication mode through colour, lighting, photographs, drawings, art and film.
- *Space* can define how objects or people relate to each other or function separately.
- *Language*, both in spoken and written form, is the dominant mode of adult life.

As adults, we are accomplished in reading these modes fluently and in combination. We are able to read subtext, respond to intent and intellectually use these skills to make meaning from a piece of music or a work of art. We are also able to resolve dissonances created by conflicting communication, for example, if stern words are delivered with a smile, we will interpret gesture as the dominant mode and not respond to the words. But for most adults, the predominant mode is language. Unless we choose to pursue an interest in music, dance, theatre or visual arts, we lose the skill of communicating personally through these media.

Young children see no such distinction, as language (particularly written language) is the last semiotic system that they master. A baby's first response in life is to sound – voices of carers. Visual perception follows and babies are able to combine the modes of sound, vision and gesture to 'read' the moods of those around them. As they grow and start to move around, they develop skills in spatial awareness, where they are in relation to objects, the direction they need to crawl or walk in to reach a desired end and how to operate as a separate entity within a space.

So by the time children start to experiment with spoken language, and years before they can read and write, children can empathise, infer, deduce, interpret actions and sounds and so understand layers of meaning. These skills are further developed through the social networking, computer and TV habits of their environment. They can 'read' films and TV programmes with growing accuracy, particularly when spoken language is mastered enough to seek clarification through questioning (the relentless 'Why?' of the toddler).

When formal education begins, children rely on these skills to navigate around, and interact with, their environment. They will move seamlessly between modes – for example, when composing music, young children will often say they are looking for a 'purple' or 'scratchy' sound. Gradually a multimodal approach to learning becomes subsumed in the need to become literate and numerate in order to find a meaningful place in society. Multimodal learning approaches become separated into subject disciplines which you are either 'good at', i.e. drawing, painting, acting or playing an instrument, or which you abandon with relief at the earliest opportunity.

For learning to be described as multimodal, it must operate within at least two different modes. Complex picture books fulfil these criteria and are widely enjoyed. However, the educational world is slower to engage with other media such as image and film. Often they are used as stimuli to writing, but not as an essential strand of literacy teaching in their own right. But children are media literate long before they are text literate, so the argument to bring this culture into the classroom is becoming increasingly persuasive.

So, in the same way that Charles Dickens used the media of his day to communicate a social message through stories, so children can interpret his stories and messages, and write the stories of their own lives, through the media of their day.

Further reading

Bearne, E. and Wolstencraft, H. (2007) *Visual Approaches to Teaching Writing: Multimodal Literacy 5–11*, London: Sage.

Cineliteracy

By the time children start school, they are usually skilled in understanding character, plot, setting, dilemma, resolution, beginning, middle and end in the many films that they will have watched. They will know good characters from bad; they can infer meaning and make predictions which are confirmed or contradicted as the plot develops. They can track shifts in time and setting, following the actions of multiple characters. They have become skilled readers of film. There are clear parallels here with the advanced text-reading and text-writing skills that they will be taught during their school life, but film is unique in that it exists in time, rather than text. As such, it should be taught and used as a separate, but linked, strand of the literacy curriculum: sitting in the director's chair is a form of authorship. The following terms can be explicitly taught when analysing film and children enjoy using accurate terminology when they are making their own films. A suggestion for the written-text equivalent follows in italics.

- *Long shot*: this is used to set the scene, or when one scene changes to another, drawing the viewer in and suggesting forward movement.
- *Wide shot*: similar intention to a long shot, but the shot is fixed in time, with no suggested movement.
  Rich, descriptive writing is used to set the scene, possibly based on what the writer can see, hear and smell: words are used to paint a picture for the reader.
- *Medium shot*: used to show characters interacting, often when significant dialogue is being exchanged.
  Dialogue is used to move the narrative forward.
- *Close-up*: used to show emotion, the detail of a character's appearance or reactions.
  Writing focuses on one aspect of a character e.g. an emotional reaction. The writer remains focused on this for several sentences, inviting reflection from the reader.
- *Low angle*: the camera is looking upwards at a character, creating an impression of power.
- *High angle*: the camera looks down on a character, making them seem small, isolated or insignificant. In both low and high angle shots, the viewer feels himself to be behind the camera and so is drawn into the image.
  Vocabulary needs to be chosen to describe feelings and possibly to explain why the character feels this way. Inferential writing skills can be developed.
- *Pan*: a fixed camera moves around slowly, allowing the viewer to take in the whole scene.
  The pace of writing is slowed by using complex sentences, inviting the reader to reflect on what is being described.

- *Tracking shot*: often used to follow a character during action.
  Writing is pacy, using short sentences and action vocabulary suggests speed.
- *Cut*: when the action suddenly cuts from one scene to another, or one camera angle to another.
  Changes of paragraph are signalled where a cut leads to a scene change.
- *Zoom*: the director wants the viewer to focus on an emotion, reaction or scene.
  Writing moves from general to specific, detailed description.

Sound is also fundamental to film. Music can communicate emotion, build or relieve tension or signal changes in pace or action. The atmosphere created by sound effects can be analysed by playing children key sections of a soundtrack alone (such as the opening) and asking them to predict what is happening. Dialogue, which moves the narrative forward in both film and text, is supported by gesture in film – this has to be described in written text. Silence has its place only in film. Children live in an image-dominated world, so focusing analytical attention on sound can yield powerful results in writing.

Colour can be used to convey character (reds and blacks for villains and bright colours or whites for heroes, or vice versa), mood, season or passing of time (sunrise and sunset, mid-day). Light also conveys meaning: spotlighting one character focuses the viewer's attention; shadow suggests concealment; darkness can engender fear.

All of these components of film need to be analysed in order for children to understand both how they have learnt to infer and deduce, and how they can communicate meaning in their own films.

Further reading

Bazalgette, C. (ed.) (2010) *Teaching Media in Primary Schools*, London: Sage.
BFI Education *Look Again!* Free download available from http://www.bfi.org.uk/education/teaching/lookagain

Visual grammar

Complex picture books are now a standard part of most classrooms and their value is understood. What is less well understood is why images are so powerful. Being able to read and understand images will help children to think more carefully about their own creative communication through image. These are some aspects of visual grammar to consider:

- *Salience*: the importance or dominance of objects or people are communicated by use of relative size, how well they are in focus, foregrounding, colour and contrast with surrounding parts of the image.
- *Vectors*: an invisible line created by the direction in which a character is looking. A demand vector is a direct gaze from the character to the reader, inviting the reader into the action. An offer vector is an indirect gaze at another character or an object, directing the reader's attention towards the same object. It can communicate information about relationships.
- *Framing*: directs the reader's attention to a chosen focus. It can be used to imply being trapped or separated. Sequential images can also be framed on one page to suggest pace in the narrative.
- *Perspective*: linked with salience or dominance, the use of perspective will force the reader to look up to characters with power and look down on small, powerless or insignificant characters.
- *Positioning*: each area of an image can create a different zone of information. The upper half of the image suggests the ideal, while the lower half suggests realism. The left half (because

of our left/right dominance in reading and writing) suggests known ground whilst the right-hand side suggests new ground. Movement from left to right suggests 'going' (known to unknown) whilst movement from right to left suggests 'return' (unknown to known ground). The central or peripheral placing of characters will also communicate information to the reader.

● *Symbolism*: symbols are rich, cultural forms of communication. Colour can be used – red could suggest blood and therefore death, or a rose-coloured red would suggest love. Shape can give information, such as a cross to suggest a religious connotation. Horizontal lines between characters suggest communication whilst vertical lines symbolise separation or division.

Further reading

Evans, J. (2009) *Talking Beyond the Page*, London: Routledge.

Kress, G. (2003) *Literacy in the New Media Age*, London: Routledge.

Kress, G. and Leeuwen, T. van (2006) *Reading Images: The Grammar of Visual Design*, London: Routledge.

Web 2.0 technologies

'Web 2.0 technologies' is a term used to describe the category of internet tools that require collaborative contribution, such as social networking sites (MSN, Facebook, Bebo, Twitter), blogs, wikis and video-sharing sites such as YouTube. Today's children are an online generation – many young people use these technologies daily and this cultural phenomenon cannot be ignored. A wide range of open source software is also available.

Consistent use of these technologies is not widespread in schools for a range of reasons. Some local authorities block social networking and all image sites for safeguarding reasons. Many parents are also apprehensive about both online activity and the validity of such media in high quality educational provision. Some schools are concerned about those children who have no computer access at home. To access some sites, children need individual email accounts, which not all schools are willing to facilitate. However, many schools are successfully using video-sharing sites, regularly Tweet about their work (this is particularly powerful for children with extended families spread around the world) and make thoughtful use of collaborative, public sites. These schools have made informed judgements about what to use rather than just ignoring all possibilities. They have discussed the issues, dealt with the practicalities, trained their children in online safety protocols and they monitor use carefully. If this is not an option, or too many sites are blocked for meaningful online use, virtual learning environments (VLEs) are safe and can emulate Web 2.0 technologies. The limitation of a VLE is that work cannot be shared outside of the learning community.

The following sites are a few that schools have found useful in social media presentations:

● http://www.wordle.net text can be scanned in and a single image is created, sizing words according to the frequency of usage

● http://www.tagxedo.com is similar to Wordle

● http://www.wallwisher.com/ allows a community to create online sticky notes when researching collaboratively

● http://www.primarywall.com/ is a similar facility for primary schools

● http://animoto.com/ images and text can be combined to create an online publication

● http://www.windowsphotostory.com is similar to animoto although it is free downloadable software which makes it particularly suitable for VLE use. Images or artwork can be combined with text, a voiceover for each image and music to create an e-book. It will need Mediaplayer 10 to run

- http://www.lulu.com does the same, but the e-books can be read and purchased publicly if you wish
- http://www.zooburst.com allows you to use your own images and photos and converts them to a pop-up book
- http://www.primarypad.com allows children to write collaboratively in real time – this can be simulated in a VLE chat room, although collaboration will be limited to the single VLE community
- http://edu.glogster.com/ short for 'graphical blog', glogster is a social media site that allows you to create an interactive poster of a character in a book or a theme
- http://www.kerpoof.com/ owned and operated by the Disney corporation, this site allows you to create your own films and share them online
- http://www.voicethread.com stores online videos and images and collaborative group conversations can be held around these
- http://www.cooliris.com is a free download which allows you to browse large numbers of images
- http://www.panoramas.dk is a collection of panoramic images from around the world. They are similar to gaming images in that the viewer appears to be standing inside the image
- http://www.aviary.com is an online image-editing facility
- http://www.podbean.com to make your own podcast.

Not all of these sites are free, but the costs involved are minimal, especially given the powerful outcomes which are possible. New possibilities emerge almost daily, so an occasional internet search can pay rich dividends.

Further reading

Richardson, W.H. (2010) *Blogs, Wikis, Podcasts and Other Powerful Web Tools for Classrooms*, Thousand Oaks, California: Corwin Press.

Drama activities

The following is a list of drama activities which can be used to develop understanding of character. Exploration through drama is a powerful activity. It brings children together to consider issues collaboratively, exposing them to multiple points of view beyond their own. It allows them to explore relationships, power, social issues, strong emotions and intent in a safe, fictional environment and so helps them to understand the social behaviours of themselves and others. Drama games develop skills of inference and deduction, calling on multiple intelligences in using space, movement, mime, gesture, sound and silence. Multimodal communication can transcend cultural barriers, allowing each participant to consider an issue both from within their own unique socio-cultural context and from outside of other contexts, without taking a critical stance on either. The deeper understanding that drama activities will give is a powerful rehearsal for writing.

Conscience alley

Use this activity when a character faces a dilemma and has to make a decision. Divide pupils into two groups who form two lines, facing each other with a central alleyway. One side has to present the arguments for one course of action. The other side has to present the opposing point of view. One person, working in role as the character with a dilemma, must walk slowly through the alley. Opposing comments are offered from each line in turn and at the end of the alley the character must decide what to do, explaining why they have made this decision. This activity could be used when Stephen Blackpool (*Hard Times*) has to decide whether to join a union and campaign with his fellow factory workers for better working conditions or whether to follow his conscience and refuse to join, which would result in being cold-shouldered by other workers.

Diary room

This requires a video camera to be available. Working in role, a character records entries on a video diary. This could be a one-off activity, or multiple entries over several sessions could track the interaction of the protagonist with others as the narrative unfolds. A video diary for Esther Summerson (*Bleak House*) could track her thoughts from her unhappy childhood, to the contentment of life at Bleak House which is shattered by smallpox and the discovery of her parentage. Her thoughts could be recorded as she reluctantly agrees to marry Mr Jarndyce, only to find lasting happiness when she is released from this engagement in order to marry the man she really loves.

Freeze frame

Working in small groups, pupils create an image similar to the single frame of a film, with action frozen in time. It focuses attention on a single aspect of a narrative, or the single emotion or reaction of a character. Body use, including arms, hands, fingers and facial expressions, has to be carefully considered. A sequence of freeze frames can be created by providing each group with a different scene to freeze. Take digital images of the frames to enhance discussion after the activity.

Heard a rumour

This is a powerful activity to use when a group of people in a story has been affected by a particular action. Without collaboration, each person has to think of a reason why this has happened, then walk around the room whispering their rumour to whomever they meet. Continue until most rumours have been widely shared, then collect the rumours for consideration. How close are the predictions to the real reason? For example, children could act in role as the servants at Chesney Wold (*Bleak House*) at the point when Lady Dedlock faints after seeing a handwritten document. They could create rumours about what was in Mr Tulkinghorn's hands which gave rise to such a reaction. It is important, when using *Heard a rumour*, that this activity takes place before children reach the point in the narrative when the real reason becomes apparent.

Hot seating

One person works in role as a character whose actions you want to explore. The character is asked questions about their actions, reactions or feelings. It can be useful, if pupils are inexperienced in hot seating, to spend some time discussing how to formulate a good question – it should be open, inviting comment and it should derive from the text. For example if David Copperfield was being hot seated, he could be asked why he thought his mother agreed to his being sent away to school.

Join the forum

After watching a freeze frame, sculptor and sculpted or any drama activity where the class watches a small group presentation, invite the class to join a forum to comment on how what they have seen has enhanced their understanding or how the work could be developed to convey deeper meaning.

Mantle of the expert

A group or an individual researches and takes on an expert role in order to understand an aspect of the story. For instance, a group could research the lives of Victorian factory workers or life in the workhouse as background to any of Dickens' novels. They could report back as a team of investigative journalists who want to bring the plight of the poor to the attention of a philanthropist such as Dr Barnardo.

Near and far

This activity explores the relationships between the central and other characters. Stand the main character centrally in the room. Assign a role, or ask each person in the group to take on the role of another character. Each person should use the space in the room to show how close their character is to the central character. Ask each person in turn why they made the decision. This could give rise to considerable discussion about changing relationships – for example, at the beginning *of A Christmas Carol*, Bob Cratchit, Tiny Tim and his family and Scrooge's nephew Fred, his only living relative, would all be distant. Only the ghosts would be near and then only for a short time. By the end of the story, the ghosts have gone and Scrooge has become the centre of Fred's and the Cratchit family's lives. A graphic representation of this could track changes in relationships over the course of the story.

Role play

You place yourself in an imagined context and explore how characters react and behave. This can be a solo or group role – for instance it could be used to explore the relationship between David Copperfield and his step-father, leading to greater understanding of why each character behaves as he does within the moral and social structures of Victorian society. When working in a group or pair, try exchanging roles to gain another perspective (role reversal). Think about body language; for example, does the characters' relationship permit eye contact? How can posture and gesture show relative positions of authority and subservience? What sort of verbal language is used in conversation – a Victorian child/adult relationship would be very different from today's relationships, even between parent and child. Experiment with the original language of the text and how phrases and sentences might be said. After working in role, writing and response activities should show more empathy with, and understanding of, character and events.

Role on the wall

Draw a large, life-sized outline of a character in the story. Then use one of the following activities, depending on what you want to investigate.

- Activity One. This supports exploration of a character's external and internal qualities. Give children two small sticky notes. First, examine the text to find the external features of the character, e.g. hair colour and length, clothing, appearance, etc. Ask each child to write one feature on a sticky note, then take it in turns to stick their note on the outside of the outline. Provide opportunities for children to read each other's comments. Then repeat this, using the text to infer or deduce the personality of the character, for example, gentle, angry, etc. Evidence should be provided for any inference. Stick these notes inside the outline to demonstrate internal characteristics.
- Activity Two. This demonstrates the centrality of a character to the story and the view of other characters. Use sticky notes to list anything that is known about the character – this could be appearance, details of the plot or what sort of person the character is. Stick these notes

inside the outline. Around the outside, list information about how other people see the character, for example, Oliver is seen as wicked by Mr Bumble, an opportunity by Fagin and a lost, lonely child by Mr Brownlow.

Sculptor and sculpted

Pupils work in pairs for this activity. One person acts as the sculptor and shapes their partner (the sculpted) to portray a particular point in the narrative where you want to explore a character's reactions. For instance, Oliver could be sculpted when he pretends to be asleep but is actually watching Fagin check his treasure trove. How could a sculpture convey both fear and shock and a sudden dawning of reality, whilst pretending to be asleep? And when the pupils swap roles, how could a sculpture of Fagin convey the sneaking, gloating pride he takes in his ill-gotten gains at the same time as portraying his suspicion of Oliver?

Teacher in role

This is a powerful form of communication. It can be used to lead role play from within a group – a teacher can take on an adult role to allow exploration of a child's perspective. If the roles are then reversed, the teacher working in role has provided an effective model of gesture, posture and tone of voice. For example, when exploring Mr Gradgrind's stern, domineering relationship with his children, his role could be taken by the teacher. Reversing this role would be challenging for pupils, who have only observational experience of the exercise of power by an adult.

Thought tracking

This can usefully take place after an activity such as *Freeze frame* or *Sculptor and sculpted*. Still in role, characters are asked to speak their thoughts aloud. This can sometimes demonstrate that a character is thinking one thing but doing something contradictory in order to hide their real thoughts.

Thought tunnel

This is similar to *Conscience alley*, but instead of the two lines of pupils presenting arguments and counter-arguments, they say aloud what they think the character might be thinking. If the character is dealing with a dilemma, this could be developed so that the conflicting thoughts of the character are presented, with one side presenting thoughts 'for' a choice and the other side presenting thoughts 'against' the choice. A thought tunnel could be used at the point in *Hard Times* when Stephen Blackpool is asked by Mr Bounderby to spy on the emerging union. To do so would leave him socially isolated and affect his relationship with Rachael, but refusing could cost him a job which he cannot afford to lose.

Further reading

Farmer, D. (2009) *101 Drama Games and Activities*, www.lulu.com.

Cremin, T., McDonald, R., Goff, E. and Blakemore, L. (2009) *Jumpstart! Drama*, London: David Fulton Publishers.

Theodorou, M. (2009) *Classroom Gems: Games, Ideas and Activities for Primary Drama*, Harlow: Longman.

2   *A Christmas Carol*

Overview

Context and social background

A Christmas Carol was written in just six weeks at the end of 1843 when Dickens was in need of money. It was an instant success and it has remained popular for more than 160 years, with its portrayal of the meaning of Christmas. During his lifetime, it was also one of his most popular books for public reading – he wrote an abridged version for performance which he read in about 90 minutes. The book is structured in five sections, called stanzas, possibly a reference to the verses of a song or carol. Ghost stories were very popular with Victorian readers, who were fascinated by supernatural powers; Wilkie Collins' 1859 novel *The Woman in White* enjoyed similar success to *A Christmas Carol.*

The debate about the Poor Law and provision of care for the poor was keenly pursued during the nineteenth century. The view of Scrooge is representative, in part, of the thinking of Thomas Malthus, who suggested that famine, poverty, war and disease were natural ways of controlling the population so that it did not grow beyond the available resources to sustain and feed it. He advocated welfare reform, disagreeing with an amendment to the Poor Law which provided more support the more children a family produced. He argued that this encouraged the poor to have more children, when fear of starvation would be more likely to prohibit large families. Scrooge articulates this view when he refuses to donate to a collection for the poor who are unwilling to enter the workhouse, saying, 'If they would rather die, they had better do it, and decrease the surplus population.'

Until the seventeenth century, Christmas was celebrated as part of twelve days of feasting, dancing and drinking which also marked the change of year. Christmas Day was defined as a holy day and the period often ended on Twelfth Night with performances of plays. Oliver Cromwell's Puritan government legislated against all holy day celebrations so Christmas lost its significance until, during the reign of Queen Victoria, the foundations of a modern Christmas were laid. Holidays were taken, as the middle classes could now afford to take two days off work. Thanks to the building of railways, families were able to get together more easily. In 1843 the first Christmas cards were sent, facilitated by the invention of the Penny Post three years earlier. This increased further in 1870 when the postage rate was halved. Also around this time, Santa Claus, stockings and the decorating of a tree became popular. Some of these traditions were introduced to England from Germany by Prince Albert and all were celebrated by the royal family. The carols which are still sung today were written in the nineteenth century and crackers were also invented. Charles Dickens is credited with further popularising Christmas with this novel.

Synopsis

Ebenezer Scrooge, a wealthy miser, hates Christmas and all that it represents. Between Christmas Eve and Christmas Day, he is visited by four ghosts. The first of these is the ghost of his former business partner, Jacob Marley, who urges him to listen to what the other spirits have to say. In turn they show him past Christmases, the coming Christmas and a future Christmas after his death. He is shown the legacy that his meanness will leave behind and he suddenly understands how his actions affect those around him. He is so moved by this that he reforms himself, celebrating expansively with his employees and family when he wakes up on Christmas morning.

Main characters

- Ebenezer Scrooge, protagonist, surviving partner of Scrooge and Marley
- The ghost of Jacob Marley, deceased partner of Scrooge and Marley
- Bob Cratchit, clerk to Scrooge
- Fred, Scrooge's nephew
- The Ghost of Christmas Past
- The Ghost of Christmas Present
- The Ghost of Christmas Yet to Come

Minor characters

- The Cratchit family, Mrs Cratchit, Martha (a milliner's apprentice), Belinda, Peter, two unnamed younger children and Tiny Tim
- Fanny, Scrooge's sister
- Mr and Mrs Fezziwig
- Dick Wilkins, a fellow apprentice when Scrooge was working for Mr Fezziwig
- Belle, Scrooge's former fiancée, now married to someone else
- Fred's unnamed wife, family and friends
- A creditor and his wife, Caroline
- Mrs Dilber, Scrooge's laundress, a charwoman and an undertaker's man
- Joe, who purchases Scrooge's possessions after his death

Settings

- The counting house of Scrooge and Marley, London
- Ebenezer Scrooge's home
- The Cratchit family home in Camden Town
- The home of Scrooge's nephew, Fred, and his wife
- Scrooge's boarding school
- A mine, a lighthouse and a ship at sea

Themes

- Christmas
- Meanness and greed
- Poverty
- Loneliness
- Family
- Change

Symbolism

- Fog and darkness
- Light
- Chains

Activities

Hooks, starters and pause points

The thinking box * / **

Put a few coins in a box with a lid so that pupils cannot see what is inside. Pupils must ask questions to establish the contents of the box. Encourage the use of higher order questioning, for example, 'What is it made from?' rather than 'Is it paper?'

When the item has been guessed, discuss the power of money – how we get money, what we do with it, what it might be like not to have any money and how money affects all of our lives. When do we have enough money? Should we help people with nothing? Can pupils think of specific examples, maybe related to their school's or community's charity work? Use the outcomes from this discussion to introduce *A Christmas Carol*. Explain that even though the novel is set over 160 years ago, the themes of rich/poor and selfishness/generosity are still relevant today.

I'm still here! * / **

Watch the clip from Robert Zemeckis' 2009 version of *A Christmas Carol* when Scrooge, trapped in his own bed curtains, realises that he is still alive (http://www.youtube.com/watch?v=znL2wyOOss0&feature=relmfu). Through shared discussion, predict the back story – what might have happened to make Scrooge so happy? Why might he be hanging upside down? Why does he feel as light as a feather?

Chains * / **

Provide pupils with several strips of paper. On each strip, they should write one fact about themselves – this could be a characteristic, a description of appearance or something about a hobby or a friend. When this has been completed (and time is the only limit on the number of statements each pupil wants to write), make the strips of paper into a paper chain. Each chain is a personal snapshot of its creator's life.

Watch a film version of the section of *A Christmas Carol* when Scrooge is visited by the ghost of Jacob Marley. Alternatively, read a suitable version aloud. What does Jacob Marley say about the chains that he and the other spirits are carrying? Why do they carry them? Can they remove them? Why not? Refer back to the pupils' chains.

Explain that the book *A Christmas Carol* describes how Scrooge, a mean, old miser, changes the links in his chain whilst he is still alive, after learning some important lessons about caring for his family and people in need. As a reinforcement activity you could return to this at the completion of the novel to make a chain for Scrooge – facts about Scrooge the miser could be written on grey or dull links and facts after he has changed could be written on brightly coloured paper to emphasise the change.

Knowledge grab * / ** / ***

The purpose of this activity is to establish prior knowledge, both to inform the teacher of an appropriate starting point and for pupils to organise their own thinking about what they already know and what they want to find out. It can be used at the start of a unit, for example to establish what pupils know about a particular aspect of Victorian society or what they know about Charles Dickens. As an individual lesson starter this activity could help to establish what is known about a character, the plot so far, or a detailed aspect of Dickens' choice and use of language.

As a plenary, it can be used to establish what has been learnt in a lesson, or at a pause point in a lesson to review what has been learnt so far. As such, it provides a means of formative assessment for the teacher in informing next steps in learning and for pupils in the process of self-evaluation of individual learning.

A ghost of an idea ***

In the Preface to *A Christmas Carol*, Dickens writes,

> I have endeavoured in this Ghostly little book, to raise the Ghost of an Idea, which shall not put my readers out of humour with themselves, with each other, with the season, or with me. May it haunt their houses pleasantly, and no one wish to lay it.

Through shared discussion, try to define what might Dickens have meant by the 'Ghost of an Idea'. With whom is he trying to raise the idea? What might he want his readers to think about? Remind pupils to note thoughts and return to this discussion at key points in the narrative to clarify, through further discussion, what the phrase might mean. Does its meaning become clearer as the novel progresses?

Word associations ** / ***

When someone says the word 'Scrooge' what do you think of? List some of the associations which are made, which will probably include words like 'miser' and 'mean'. Review the word list – are all the words negative?

Then think about the Victorian readers of *A Christmas Carol*. They had no knowledge of the characteristics that Scrooge represented, so how would their expectations of the novel differ from a contemporary reader's? Might they be familiar with a nineteenth-century figure on whom Scrooge was based?

Face-off ** / ***

It is important when considering characterisation to understand how interaction between characters gives the reader information. Use *Face-off* as a lesson starter when considering interaction. Brainstorm different ways of communicating – people can be polite, abrupt, kind, warm, funny, etc. The way a person speaks often determines the reactions of those around them.

Pupils should work in pairs. The first person says something in a particular way, using one of the ideas from the brainstorm. How is the second person going to react? In particular, consider the choices which we have when faced with blunt comments such as Scrooge's 'Bah, humbug!' We can remain polite, we can answer in kind or we can be cheerful. Each different response says something about the respondent and also about the relationship between the people involved in the conversation.

A face-off can also be used as an improvisation at a pause point where you want pupils to analyse character interaction. It not only allows pupils to think in role, but also gives the teacher an insight into pupils' understanding. As an additional challenge, ask pupils to use Dickens' language when working in role.

What's going on? ***

Use this as a lesson starter after a particular part of the text has been read. Group or pair pupils to prepare one statement based on the text. The class has to decide if this statement is true or false, using evidence from the text to explain their view.

Statements can involve basic fact retrieval, for example, 'Bob Cratchit lives in Camden Town' or a statement which requires the use of inference or deduction skills to decide if it is true or false. For example in Stave 1 a statement could read 'Scrooge did not care what people thought of him'. This is true, as not only did he not care, but the text states that it was the way he preferred to live: 'It was the very thing he liked. To edge his way along the crowded path of life, warning all humanity to keep its distance.' Alternatively, a statement such as 'Bob Cratchit was scared of his employer' cannot be clearly categorised – when Fred finished his speech, Bob applauded even though it annoyed Scrooge. However, he dared not collect more coal for his waning fire, as 'so surely as the clerk came in with the shovel, the master predicted that it would be necessary for them to part'.

This activity will also give insight into the depth at which each individual pupil is engaging with the text.

Your number's up ** / ***

Ask a pupil to choose a number between one and ten. The pupil then has to give a corresponding number of facts about a topic which you suggest. This could be a character that has been studied, the plot or the social or historical context of the novel. This continues until all pupils have contributed or all known facts have been recalled. This can also be used as a plenary or by dividing the class into groups of ten, so that there are more opportunities to contribute. In this case, pupils should provide the facts to their group. As a further challenge when recalling facts from the narrative, ask for evidence from the text to be provided to support the given fact. At the completion of the activity, pupils can evaluate their own knowledge.

States of mind ** / ***

Use this to introduce a lesson which is considering the state of mind of a particular character. Challenge pupils to find as many ways as possible of silently communicating a given emotion. Facial expressions, hand gestures, posture, limb position and occupation of space and body proximity to other characters should all be considered.

Instead of portraying the state of mind of a given character, the activity could be reversed so that pupils communicate a state of mind and others in the class have to work out which character is being portrayed. Discuss how the answer was determined and what information from the text was being used both by the actors and the viewers.

States of mind can also be used at key pause points in the course of a lesson, for example, when tracking changes in states of mind. Use digital images of each pose to compare how the character's reactions have changed in the course of the section of the plot which is being studied.

Just one word ** / ***

Ask pupils to choose one word to summarise what the reader might feel about Scrooge at any given point in the story. The challenge is to find a quotation which reinforces the viewpoint. For example, after the visit of Marley's Ghost, the word 'sceptical' could be chosen in summary. The quotation to support that word choice would be 'You may be an undigested bit of beef, a blot of mustard, a crumb of cheese, a fragment of an underdone potato. There's more of gravy than of grave about you, whatever you are!' The arrival of the final spirit could be summarised as 'contrition' because Scrooge says, 'I fear you more than any spectre I have seen. But as I know your purpose is to do me good … I am prepared to bear you company, and do it with a thankful heart.'

Literary devices ***

Resource 2.1 (*Literary devices*) contains a cloze exercise in order to secure pupils' understanding of narrative techniques. These definitions should be revisited throughout the study of the novel. As an activity, pupils could find examples of different narrative techniques and discuss the effect of each example on the reader.

Just a minute ***

This activity can be used to review knowledge at any point in a lesson. As a lesson starter, pupils can be invited to talk about a particular character, a setting or an aspect of plot or structure, for one minute. As an extra challenge, can this be done without the speaker pausing or repeating themselves? Are all comments relevant to the topic? This also offers the opportunity for formative, ongoing assessment.

Just a minute can also be used in a debate format, when pupils need to consider opposing points of view. A pupil must talk about a given issue for one minute (including the challenge rules where appropriate), and then their partner must rebut this viewpoint by presenting a different point of view. In both cases, evidence from the text should be provided to support each point of debate.

Understanding character

Painting with words: 1 * / **

> **Objectives**
> - to explore how an author uses descriptive language to create images in the mind of the reader
> - to understand how appearance is used to represent character.

Dickens used words to paint pictures in the minds of his readers. But not only do these words paint pictures of appearances, they also represent the characteristics of the people being described. Using text extract 2.1 (*The Three Christmas Spirits*) read aloud Dickens' description of the Ghost of Christmas Past, using the paraphrase if more appropriate to the age and experience of the class. Ask pupils to note key words as they listen. Display the text and, through shared discussion, mark key words. Discuss what this tells the reader about the appearance of the Ghost. Ask pupils to draw, then colour, the picture which the description creates in their own mind. To evaluate the completed images, compare similarities across the images. How powerful are Dickens' words in painting the original picture in the readers' mind? With older pupils, discuss how appearance represents an aspect of the story – Christmas Past represents memory, Christmas Present represents generosity and goodwill to all men, whilst Christmas Yet to Come represents fear of the future and the loneliness of death.

This can then be repeated with the Ghost of Christmas Present and the Ghost of Christmas Yet to Come. Alternatively, study the three extracts before creating the images and allow pupils to choose which ghost image they wish to reproduce, evaluating them against the text extracts when complete. These images could then be produced as models if a film option is to be pursued.

Whilst working, it can be inspiring to listen to music – the following suggestions are all readily available:

- The Ghost of Christmas Past
  - *Impossible Opening* from *Finding Neverland: Jan A.P. Kaczmarek*
  - *Le Onde: Ludovico Einaudi*
  - *Ladies in Lavender: Teaching Andrea* and *Fantasy for Violin and Orchestra* from *Ladies in Lavender: Nigel Hess*
- The Ghost of Christmas Present
  - *Rondeau* from *Abdelazar: Henry Purcell*
  - *Crown Imperial: William Walton*
- The Ghost of Christmas Yet to Come
  - *Symphony No. 3, Sorrowful Songs, 2nd movement: Henryk Gorecki*
  - *Song for Athene: John Tavener*

Painting with words: 2 * / **

> **Objective**
> - to respond to descriptive prose and images by writing poetry.

This activity provides an opportunity to respond to the ghost images through writing poetry. Using a fast poem structure (Corbett, 2005: 25) select one noun, two adjectives, three adverbs and four verbs to make an effective poem. Resource 2.2 (*How to write a fast poem*) is a PowerPoint which models the steps taken in writing the following fast poems.

Ghost
Smooth and strong,
Softly, gently, invisibly,
Swirling, shining, sparkling, dissolving.

Giant
Radiant and enthroned.
Genially, gloriously, joyfully,
Gleaming, glistening, glowing, laughing.

Can pupils tell which ghost is being described? Can they repeat this with each other's poems? This should be possible if effective word choices have been made. Encourage older pupils to think about words which represent the character of each ghost, not just the appearance. An example of this would be:

Death
Dark and abandoned.
Silently, slowly, solemnly,
Concealing, pointing, shrouding, approaching.

Families at Christmas * / **

> **Objective**
> ● to investigate how authors portray relationships within a context.

Conveying relationships through dialogue is a key authorship skill. This activity explores how Dickens' characters communicate within one family (the Cratchits) and attempts to analyse what the reader learns about the family from the narrative. Text extract 2.2 describes the *Cratchit Family Christmas*. For older pupils, this can be used to write and perform a play script of their own. A play script is available as resource 2.3 if you wish to limit this activity to performance or scaffold pupils' writing using a sample text.

Before starting to read the play script, spend some time discussing how families communicate – consider body language, eye contact and style of language used. Are conversations between adults different from those between adults and children? How do siblings talk to each other? What does this tell an observer about how members of a family feel about each other?

Rehearse and perform the scene, conveying the family atmosphere. Either video and analyse the performances, or use the class as an audience to comment on how effectively each performance has portrayed the warmth and humour of the Cratchit family. Complete the activity by discussing the following questions.

From watching and performing this scene, using words, phrases and evidence from the script to support your view:

● What sort of relationship did the family have?
● How does the author use dialogue to show that these people are close and know each other well?
● How do you think poverty affected the family?

Sculptor and sculpted with thought tracking * / **

> **Objective**
> ● to understand how a character's behaviour and attitudes change over time in response to the actions of others.

At the end of each section of the story, discuss what Scrooge was thinking and how we know. For example, when his nephew called in to wish him a merry Christmas, Scrooge responded with his famous phrase, 'Bah! Humbug!' What does this tell us about his view of Christmas?

Text extract 2.3 (*Thought tracking Scrooge*) contains ten sections from the narrative which are key points in tracking Scrooge's thinking. Read through the extracts and decide what Scrooge is thinking at each point. Then divide the class into ten groups, giving each group one card from resources 2.4 or 2.5 (differentiated *Sculptor and sculpted*). With one person in each group representing Scrooge, others should sculpt Scrooge into a statue which shows his attitude at the point of the story that the card describes. Some key words are provided. Encourage pupils to think carefully about body language, including what is communicated by head (looking up, head hanging in shame), arm and hand position, posture (upright or slouching) and facial expression. Change the role of sculptor and statue until the group is satisfied with the sculpture. At this point, take a digital image. Use the information in the Cineliteracy section of Chapter 1 for details about enhancing the images.

Older pupils could thought track as an extension activity – when the statue is finished, ask the person to speak in role as Scrooge, saying what he is thinking. A video camera should be used if thought tracking is included.

When the activity is complete, review the images or video. What do we learn about Scrooge? How does his behaviour change? How do his actions change? What about his attitude to poverty and suffering? Is there any wider knowledge from the text which can be added to re-inforce the views of pupils (for example, his change towards Tiny Tim and his possible death)? List and retain ideas and vocabulary for the writing activity.

Divide pupils into pairs. Working in role as Fred, one person must use the information gained from the above activity to persuade the other person, in role as Scrooge, to join him for Christmas Day. This can be repeated with roles reversed. Then, bringing everything together, ask pupils to write a letter in role as Fred, trying to persuade Scrooge to join him the next day. A sample text is provided (resource 2.6 *Dear Uncle Scrooge*) to model the task for pupils, or for shared reading. As an additional challenge, pupils could write a letter to Scrooge trying to persuade him to join them for their own family Christmas celebrations.

The Spirit of Christmas * / **

Objective
- to track and explain the changes in a character across a text.

Read text extract 2.4 *The Spirit of Christmas* together. Through shared discussion, decide what Scrooge might have looked like. Pupils could look at images in Marcia Williams' *Oliver Twist and Other Great Dickens Stories* (2002) to support this discussion. Then ask pupils to draw a small picture of Scrooge. To expand this activity for older children, create additional images for Fred and Bob Cratchit from Dickens' descriptions of them.

As you read or tell the story, pause at key points to place Scrooge (and any other characters whom you wish to use) on *The Spirit of Christmas spectrum* (resource 2.7). As the story progresses, listeners will create a visual picture of Scrooge's journey from miser to benefactor – resources 2.4 and 2.5 show key points in the text. Will the initial image of Scrooge be appropriate for the end of the story? How will it need to change and what will effect this change? Where in the narrative do changes take place? You could put images of each ghost above the line to mark key points. Why do some characters remain in the same place throughout the narrative? Enlarge the tracking sheet onto A3 paper and track the journey as a whole class.

As a further response activity, storyboard and caption *A Christmas Carol* to show the gradual change with each ghostly visit. Two templates are provided as resource 2.8 (*The Spirit of Christmas storyboard*). As a rehearsal for the storyboarding, ask pupils to re-tell a section of the story and then draw the picture, taking it in turns to recall each section. Finally, pupils can caption their images to create the story as a picture book. Stick each storyboard onto card and tape all the cards together in a concertina pattern. This will then create *A zig-zag Christmas Carol* to be shared with other classes and family members.

Near and far **

Objective

● to consider how one character's behaviour and attitudes affect those around him.

The purpose of this activity is to understand how Scrooge's relationships with those around him changed as his attitudes also changed. Start with everyone standing in a circle, with one person representing Scrooge in the centre of the circle. Choose one person to represent each of the characters in the novel and give them a card with their character's name on. After shared discussion, decide where each character should stand in relation to Scrooge, depending on how close the character was to him emotionally. Repeat this for each stave, taking a digital image of each one.

Compare the five images – what do they show about the relationship of the characters to Scrooge? How do the relationships change during the course of the novel?

Stave 1

● Bob Cratchit
● Fred
● the two gentlemen collecting for the poor
● the boy who tried to sing a carol at his door
● people who lived in his neighbourhood

Stave 2

● Fanny, Scrooge's sister
● Mr and Mrs Fezziwig
● Dick Wilkins
● Belle

Stave 3

● Mrs Cratchit
● Tiny Tim and the Cratchit children
● Fred
● Fred's wife, family and friends

Stave 4

● business gentlemen who are discussing Scrooge's death
● Mrs Dilber, Scrooge's laundress, a charwoman and an undertaker's man
● Joe, who purchases Scrooge's possessions after his death
● the Cratchit family after the death of Tiny Tim
● a creditor and his wife, Caroline

Stave 5

● one of the gentlemen collecting for the poor
● people in Scrooge's neighbourhood
● Fred and his wife
● the guests at Fred's party
● Bob Cratchit

- Mrs Cratchit
- Tiny Tim and the Cratchit children

Scrooge spider diagram ***

> **Objective**
> - to track the development of Scrooge's character through the course of the narrative.

After reading the opening of the novel, create a spider diagram for Scrooge. Note on the diagram key characteristics about him which are revealed through his interaction with other characters. In Stave 1, for example, information can be collected from his interactions with Bob Cratchit, Fred, the charity collectors and the ghost of Jacob Marley. In later staves, this should include each of the Ghosts in turn. Brief quotations to support each entry could also be included. Ask pupils to decide at the outset of this activity whether Scrooge is intriguing or abominable. What evidence in the text leads them to their conclusion? Repeat this discussion at key points in the study to explore how the readers' views of Scrooge evolve as the narrative develops.

At the conclusion of the study, the spider diagram will give a complete overview of the development of Scrooge's character through his interactions with those around him. How do the entries at the end of the narrative differ from those at the beginning, particularly in his interaction with Fred? What does this tell the reader about the development of the character of Scrooge?

Character interaction ***

> **Objective**
> - to examine how Dickens develops the character of Scrooge through his interactions with other people.

Use this activity after reading Stave 1 to the point where the charity collectors leave and Scrooge is '*in a more facetious temper than was usual with him*'. Through shared discussion as a whole class, analyse Scrooge's conversations with his clerk. Consider the tiny fire which the clerk is allowed and Scrooge's reaction to Bob clapping when Fred finishes his speech. What do these interactions tell the reader about Scrooge's character and his view of his clerk?

Next, divide the class into two groups. One group should consider Scrooge's interaction with his nephew, Fred, and the other group should consider Scrooge's interaction with the charity collectors. Support views with quotations from the text. Then ask pupils to pair so that there is one person with information about Fred and one person with information about the charity collectors in each pair. Share ideas, challenging each other's views and using evidence from the text to support conclusions.

Finally, write a paragraph explaining what Dickens shows the reader about Scrooge's character through his interaction with others. Include quotations to support any statements which are made.

In the director's chair ***

Objective
- to interrogate a text in order to deepen understanding of how language is used to communicate character.

Provide pupils with a copy of text extract 2.5 *The director's chair*, which contains the discussion between Scrooge and Marley. This could be the whole conversation, or it could be split into sections, with each pair working on one section. Each pair of pupils should discuss how they would direct the scene if they were filming it. This would include where the characters stand in relation to each other, what kind of movements would be made or when a character is motionless. Scripts should be annotated to show all of the direction detail, as if the script was going to be given to an actor. Direction should include the narrator's comments about Scrooge's attitude, feelings and reaction.

Pupils should then form groups to discuss and share ideas. If the script has been split into sections, pupils should work with those who have studied the same section. Ask pupils to challenge each other's decisions, using evidence and quotations from the text to justify the direction which they have marked on their scripts.

Emotive language ***

Objective
- to investigate the use of emotive language by an author when creating a fully rounded character.

Using text extract 2.6 (*Emotive language*) read the sample extract, which is taken from one of the scenes which Scrooge is shown by the Ghost of Christmas Past. Using this sample, model how to interrogate the text to help the reader understand more about Scrooge's character.

Then ask pupils to do the same using the four extracts. To what extent do these quotations help the reader to understand Scrooge as a more rounded character than the person shown in Stave 1? Why has Dickens chosen this point in his narrative to introduce these more sympathetic aspects of Scrooge's character? In what ways is the reader supported in forming new conclusions? Annotate sheets with ideas and then, through shared class discussion, extend thinking further. Add any new ideas from the class discussion to resource sheets. Encourage pupils to use exploratory questions to challenge each other's thinking, including requesting evidence from the text. Next, grouping pupils, ask them to interrogate the language that Dickens has used in these descriptions. What emotions have been conveyed in each scene and how has language been used to do this? Discuss this in two contexts – the effect of the emotion on Scrooge and its effect on the reader. Encourage pupils to use quotations and evidence from the text to explicate their thinking. Finally, ask pupils to make individual responses by writing a paragraph which explains how Dickens' use of language allows the reader to understand Scrooge as a more rounded character.

Fatally flawed ***

> **Objective**
> ● to investigate how the structure of the novel helps the reader to see Scrooge as a fully rounded character.

The purpose of this activity is to consider how Dickens structures the narrative in such a way that a complete picture of the protagonist is created. Through shared discussion, define the concept of a character being fatally flawed. All characters possess flaws in order for them to be realistic and believable but a fatally flawed character cannot be redeemed and becomes the victim of his flaws.

Divide the class into five groups and assign one stave to each group. Using the relevant section of the text and all available knowledge about Scrooge acquired in the course of the study, find evidence for Scrooge being a fatally flawed character. Is there a possibility that he was simply misunderstood?

Understanding plot

Party time! * / **

> **Objective**
> ● to understand the role of the family in a Victorian Christmas.

The Victorians created the family-centred style of Christmas celebration which we still enjoy today. Dickens often read his books, or extracts from them, aloud. Start this activity by reading aloud the accounts of two Christmas parties in *A Christmas Carol* (text extract 2.7 *Party time*). The first visit which Scrooge made was in the company of the Ghost of Christmas Past, when he was reminded of an exciting party thrown by Mr Fezziwig, with whom Scrooge was apprenticed. The second was with the Ghost of Christmas Present, when he was a silent witness at the party of his nephew, Fred.

After reading these extracts aloud, discuss the dancing and games which everyone enjoyed. Learn and play some of the games listed below – some are mentioned in the text and some are favourite Victorian parlour games which would have been popular with families at Christmas.

● Blind Man's Buff: One person is blindfolded. Everyone moves around the room whilst the blindfolded person tries to catch someone. When a person is caught they must be identified by the Blind Man. The blindfold is then passed on and the game is repeated.
● Charades: Divide the group into teams. Each team is given a word to act out, a book or a book character. Films, TV and DVDs didn't exist!
● How, why, when and where: One person thinks of an object and everyone else must guess what the object is. Four questions can be asked – 'How do you like it?', 'Why do you like it?', 'When do you like it?' or 'Where do you like it?' Each player may only ask one question. The winner is the person who correctly guesses the object.
● Pass the slipper: Everyone sits in a circle with one person in the middle. The central person closes their eyes while a slipper is passed around the circle behind each person's back. The slipper stops when the person in the centre opens their eyes and tries to guess who is

ST MARY'S UNIVERSITY COLLEGE

A COLLEGE OF THE QUEEN'S UNIVERSITY OF BELFAST

holding it. If the guess is correct, the person holding the slipper moves to the centre. If the guess is wrong, the game is repeated.

- Shadows, or Shadow Buff: Darken the room, suspend a white sheet and place a light source such as a torch behind the sheet (the Victorians would have used a candle). One person sits in front of the sheet and has to identify each other person in turn as they walk between the light source and the sheet, creating a shadow. The better the distortion created by bending, stretching or making an unusual shape, the harder it is to guess.
- Spin the trencher: A wooden plate or trencher is placed on the floor in the centre of a circle of chairs. All but one person sit on a chair each. The person left standing must spin the trencher and call out the name of someone sitting on a chair. This person must catch the trencher before it falls. If they fail to do so, they pay a forfeit, their seat is taken and they become the next person in the middle. The trick is not to call a name until the trencher has almost stopped.
- The laughing game: Everyone sits in a circle. The first person says, 'Ha'. The second person says, 'Ha, ha', the third, 'Ha, ha, ha' and so on, around the circle. Anyone who laughs or smiles is out. The winner is the person who can keep a straight face for the longest.
- The sculptor: One person is chosen to be a sculptor, moving around the room and shaping each person into an awkward or amusing pose which must be held. The first person to laugh becomes the next sculptor.
- Yes and no: One person thinks of something and everyone else has to find out what it is by asking questions which can only be answered with the words 'Yes' and 'No'. The winner is the first person to guess the item correctly.

Video the games being played or take digital images, concentrating on interaction. Look at and talk about the images before and whilst using resource 2.9 *Party time discussion* for a shared discussion. Divide the class into groups and allow five minutes to discuss the questions. In each group, a scribe notes answers and ideas. After five minutes, an envoy from each group should take their answers and visit each of the other groups in turn. At each table, the envoy shares one key point from their own group and notes down one key point from the group that he or she is visiting. To encourage thinking skills, one exploratory question can also be asked of the envoy, for example, 'Why did your group think . . . ?' When the rotation of envoys is complete, return to the original groups and share new ideas.

Through whole class discussion, fill in the Venn diagram (resource 2.10 *Party time feedback*) to show the similarities and differences between Victorian and modern parties.

Word wall **

> **Objective**
> - to demonstrate understanding of a character and the development of the character in the course of the narrative.

Use a display board or cover part of a wall in paper to create a word or graffiti wall. Starting at one end of the wall, pupils can write on it any words or phrases which describe Scrooge. These can be words which they read or hear read to them from text samples, or any words or descriptions of their own about Scrooge at the point in the story which you have reached. As the narrative unfolds, move along the wall to add new words: the nature of the words being written will change. When the story is finished, compare the words at one end of the wall, which are words from the beginning of the story, with the words chosen at the end. What does this say about the changes in Scrooge? What message was Dickens trying to communicate in the book? How well does the word wall suggest that he achieved this? Can pupils then see, from analysing the word wall, how and where the changes gradually happened and why the book was structured in the way that it was?

Extra! Extra! **

> **Objective**
> ● to write a newspaper article in role as a Victorian journalist.

Using all the information gathered in the course of studying *A Christmas Carol*, create a newspaper page about Scrooge's change of heart. The paper is to be published on Boxing Day, the morning after Scrooge shows that he is reformed. An understanding of the plot and Scrooge's transformation are necessary. A sample text to use in modelled writing is available as resource 2.11 *Extra! Extra!*

Whoosh ** / ***

> **Objective**
> ● to familiarise pupils with events of a section of the narrative.

This activity is useful for introducing pupils to the key events of a large section of a story prior to a more detailed study of the narrative, or to enable pupils to gain an overview of plot and events without reading the complete text individually. Everyone participates and it is a very active way of engaging with text and bringing it to life. It was named and is widely used in the education programmes of the Royal Shakespeare Company. Use resource 2.12 for this *Whoosh*.

Seat pupils in a circle and assign roles for the first section of the *Whoosh*. All of the text which is in bold requires some sort of action, so pupils might be representing a character (such as Scrooge) or an object (such as a door) in a pose in the centre of the circle. Sound effects can be made by everyone in chorus. Key dialogue is also included, with dialogue prompts to distribute to the pupils representing those characters. Read the *Whoosh*, with pupils adding poses, dialogue and actions to match. When you say 'Whoosh', everyone has to return to their original place in the circle. This could be as marked at the end of a section, if the circle starts to become too crowded or as a pause point.

Tension graph ***

> **Objective**
> ● to examine narrative techniques.

The control of tension in a novel is a narrative technique which affects the emotions of the reader. Introduce the definitions of rising and falling tension to pupils and examine resource 2.13 *Tension graph*. Discuss how this can be used to create a tension graph for Stave 1. How does Dickens control the rise and fall of tension in order to communicate the most important points of the narrative? Complete a graph for each stave.

Ghost comparison table ***

Objective
● to compare the role of each ghost in the narrative.

Resource 2.14 is a *Ghost comparison table* which can be completed as the book is studied. Consider the appearance and personality of each spirit, together with the events and tone of the visit. Quotations or evidence from the text should be used to support each point. At the completion of the study, analyse the comparison table. What does it say about Dickens' use of the spirits to give the narrative direction and structure? How do the interactions of the ghosts with Scrooge effect the change which is the theme of the book?

Understanding setting

Family meals at Christmas * / **

Objective
● to understand how a writer from a different time presents an experience.

This activity is also used in *Great Expectations* so could be linked in a cross-textual study of Dickens' descriptions of Victorian Christmas meals. A theme plan entitled *Celebrating Christmas* is available on the accompanying CD.

The Cratchit family is an example of how poor people celebrated Christmas in Victorian times. It was a family celebration and the sort of food which we eat today was starting to become popular. Roast turkey was eaten by those who could afford it, or roast goose by those who could not. Mince pies and Christmas puddings were also eaten. Queen Victoria is attributed with popularising these foods.

Read text extract 2.8 *The Cratchits' Christmas dinner*, which describes the meal. What does the reader learn about what poor people ate at Christmas? What examples can pupils find of figurative language: a simile (*like a speckled cannon ball*), hyperbole or exaggeration (*The youngest Cratchits, in particular, were steeped in sage and onion to the eyebrows!*), alliteration (*hissing hot*) and onomatopoeia (*sputtered and cracked*)? What effect does this have on the reader? Using this information, create a menu card for the Cratchit Christmas dinner. As an extension activity, pupils could write a descriptive paragraph about, or create their own menu card for, a celebration meal they have enjoyed, using figurative language.

Creating a setting **

Objectives
● to explore how writers use language to create effect
● to use imagination to create suspense.

Read aloud text extract 2.9 *Creating a setting* from the first stave of the book. What are the first impressions? Which words created that impression? Explain to pupils that they are going to explore the text to find out how Dickens creates the setting for *A Christmas Carol* by the way pictures are painted in the reader's mind to generate suspense. Provide each pupil with a copy of the text to mark, finding examples of the following figurative language:

- simile
- alliteration
- personification
- repetition
- noun and expanded noun phrases
- powerful verbs
- varied sentence lengths.

The writing in these paragraphs is very rich – for example, the sentence '*The owner of one young nose, gnawed by the hungry cold as bones are gnawed by dogs*', contains personification of the cold ('hungry cold') as part of a simile, with repetition.

Through shared discussion, explore the richness of this writing. What is the writer trying to create in the reader's or listener's mind? How soon does the reader realise that this is going to be a ghost story? And how has the language prior to this point contributed to the building of suspense? How many references are there to the cold? Read the extract aloud once more, asking pupils to visualise what the passage is describing.

Finally, challenge pupils to write their own story opening, using rich language to create a picture in the minds of their readers. Read the story openings aloud and evaluate. There is a short story writing activity at the conclusion of the study of *A Christmas Carol*, so pupils could retain their story opening to use as part of a complete story.

Victorian London ** / ***

> **Objective**
> - to explore the context and setting of Dickens' London.

Start by comparing a map of Victorian London such as http://charlesdickenspage.com/dickens_london_map.html with a contemporary map http://mapsof.net/uploads/static-maps/london_detailed_road_map.png. What do pupils notice? Brainstorm any differences which have been observed.

Working in pairs, make an internet search for images of Victorian London – Google Images is a rich resource for this activity. List all the information which you can find about living conditions, transport, housing, clothing, etc. From these images and the lists, discuss how life has changed since Victorian times. Has it changed for better or for worse? Then, considering Victorian living and working conditions, ask pupils to predict what themes might be included in a novel written in Victorian times by someone who wanted to comment on social conditions in his home city of London.

Settings and structure ***

> **Objective**
> ● to examine how setting can be designed to structure a narrative and communicate viewpoint.

List the settings of the novel, for example, Scrooge's office, the street as people prepared for Christmas, Scrooge's home, the Cratchits' home, etc. Each different setting is crafted to create an atmosphere appropriate to a particular point. In each case, decide through shared group discussion how Dickens used settings to make socio-cultural statements to his reader. For example, the coldness of the office is described in great detail. This reflects the coldness of Scrooge's character but also creates an appropriate setting into which to deliver the Malthusian view held by a section of Victorian society that the poor should not be supported, as starvation offered a useful form of population and birth control. Scrooge articulates it in his comment to the charity collectors that if the poor 'would rather die' than enter the workhouse, then 'they had better do it, and decrease the surplus population'.

Investigate the message which each of the other settings is designed to enhance.

Whole text responses

Short story writing **

> **Objective**
> ● to write a short story using a known classic text as a model.

Using the knowledge and understanding of characterisation, plot and structure from studying *A Christmas Carol*, write a short ghost story using Dickens' structure. The protagonist should move from one position to another with ghosts representing past, present and future to facilitate the change and the time shifts. Differentiated planning structures are suggested in resource 2.15 *A Short Ghost Story*. When the stories are complete, find an audience to read them to – remember, Dickens often read his stories aloud, too!

*Storysack® ** / ****

> **Objective**
> ● to show understanding of a complete text, using different techniques to make a text come alive.

Make a Storysack® or a story box for *A Christmas Carol*. These are very popular with younger children; the purpose is to encourage people to share a book, bringing it alive by exploring resources. A Storysack® is a large cloth bag or box, with the title of the book displayed on the front. Inside the bag or box, place a copy of the story in book and CD format and some other titles related to Christmas in Victorian times, or titles about the author. This could prompt a great deal of discussion about suitability of different versions of the story and film for different age groups as they are compared.

Props could also be included – what characters in the story might a younger child want to role play? How could this be facilitated? Could masks be made – one for each main character, or just two masks, one happy, one sad? How could children be encouraged to use them? If films have been made as an outcome, these could be included, as could models of the characters or their pictures pasted onto card, for the story to be retold in a child's own words. Or make finger or stick puppets to create an instant cast. Could simple scene boards be made?

Put in some paper, crayons and art materials so that children can create their own responses, or maybe some old Christmas cards for collage. Make and appropriately decorate some activity cards, suggesting how the resources could be used. Finally, find some children to share the sacks with and evaluate how pupils' learning about the novel has been reinforced through the creation of a Storysack®.

Film **

Objective
- to demonstrate a multimodal response to a text.

Because there are a limited number of characters in *A Christmas Carol*, making a film as a final outcome is easily achievable. The story is in five sections so five groups of pupils could opt to film one section each, or pupils could film the complete story. Pupils can choose how to create characters (card, modelling clay, Lego® or another medium) and how to create scenery or backdrops. Plan the film using a storyboard and use as much of Dickens' dialogue as possible for the script. Watch the films and review what has been learnt from the experience about the settings and characters in *A Christmas Carol*. How has film deepened pupils' understanding of the narrative?

Share a view * / **

Objectives
- to reflect critically on the understanding of a narrative
- to make a personal response to a known text.

A range of book review sheets is available as resource 2.16. Alternatively, using your VLE or a shared site such as primaryblogger.co.uk, write and post reviews of *A Christmas Carol*. A good review, whether written on paper or electronically, should say something about the aspects of plot, character and setting that the reader enjoyed most, whether the reader would recommend the book to someone else and, if so, an indication of the age, and possibly the gender, of those who would also enjoy the book. Ways in which the book has come to life, or made the reader think, would also be interesting to others. Reviews can be negative, although reasons should always be given.

The film review ***

There are a number of film versions of *A Christmas Carol*, five of which are listed below. Each time a new stave is studied, use a different film version to watch the stave. The films can be used in any order.

- *A Christmas Carol* (1951) Alastair Sim, Sir Michael Hordern, George Cole

- *A Christmas Carol* (1999) (PG) Patrick Stewart, Hugh E. Grant
- *A Muppet Christmas Carol* (2005) (U) Michael Caine
- *A Christmas Carol* (2007) (PG) Kelsey Grammer
- *A Christmas Carol* (2009) (PG) Jim Carrey

Whilst watching the films, pupils should analyse and make notes on the truthfulness of the film to Dickens' original narrative. They should also consider the accuracy of interpretation. When one stave has been viewed from each film and the study of *A Christmas Carol* is complete, decide, through shared class discussion, which film version is the most truthful interpretation of Dickens' novel. Encourage pupils to look back through notes made at each stage to support their viewpoint. Check the criteria which the pupils are using to make their judgements, asking for justification of choices against each of the criteria.

Watch the complete film which is judged to be the best interpretation. What are the messages of the chosen film? How accurate are these to Dickens' intentions in writing the novel? Can the phrase 'Ghost of an Idea' be finally defined?

After examining some samples of film reviews, ask pupils to review the preferred film of *A Christmas Carol* in a medium of their choice. Consideration of the truthfulness of interpretation should form a part of the review, together with some comment on the relevance of Victorian literature to a contemporary audience.

Reader reaction ***

Objective
- to consolidate understanding of the effect of narrative techniques on the reader.

Resource 2.17 *Reader reaction* is a table on which pupils can record their reactions to Scrooge as each stave progresses. Feelings and viewpoints should be supported with quotations. When the table is complete, share ideas and feelings. In what ways are they similar? In what ways do viewpoints differ? What narrative techniques did Dickens use to provoke the reactions which have been noted?

⊙⊙⊙ Linked reading

The Lighthouse Keeper's Christmas: Ronda Armitage and David Armitage, Scholastic.
How the Grinch Stole Christmas: Dr Seuss, Harper Collins Children's Books.
Horrible Christmas (Horrible Histories): Terry Deary and Martin Brown, Scholastic.
The Christmas Eve Ghost: Shirley Hughes, Walker.
Tim Burton's Nightmare Before Christmas: adapted by Frank Thompson, Disney.
The Christmas Miracle of Jonathan Toomey: Susan Wojciechowski and Patrick Lynch, Walker.
Looking for JJ: Anne Cassidy, Point.
The Death Defying Pepper Roux: Geraldine McCaughrean, OUP.

3 *Bleak House*

Overview

Context and social background

This novel was published in twenty illustrated instalments between 1852 and 1853. At the peak of its sales of the serialised *Bleak House* the magazine sold up to 40,000 copies. Advertising linked to content provided a rich revenue source for the publishers – for example, one edition carried advertisements for sale of equipment for an army officer.

There are two strands to the narrative, which alternates between the first person account of Esther Summerson, one of the novel's characters, and an un-named narrator who provides commentary, moving the plot forward and introducing characters into the settings from which Esther is absent. Dickens' view of the law, formed by his experience as a court reporter, is clear in this novel, which is based on a true case which lasted for 53 years, eventually leaving the inheritors bankrupt. The setting for the legal proceedings is the Court of Chancery, which dealt with all disputes about wills and inheritance. In the Preface, Dickens describes how a Chancery judge actually told him on one occasion that the popular view of Chancery was merely public prejudice. Dickens goes on to state that 'everything set forth in these pages concerning the Court of Chancery is substantially true', also saying that the case of Gridley is a true case, 'in no essential altered from one of actual occurrence'. At the time of writing *Bleak House*, there was a twenty-year-old case which had already cost £70,000 and involved thirty or forty lawyers, together with another case commenced 'before the close of the last century' (he was writing in August 1853) which was nowhere near conclusion but which had already consumed more than £140,000. Dickens uses this as proof that the problems with the Court of Chancery had nothing to do with public prejudice.

Social commentary is provided, with the lives of the rich and poor in Victorian society sharply contrasted. Poor parenting is also a key theme. Lady Dedlock abandons her daughter to be brought up by a sister who never fails to remind Esther of her unspoken shame – a comment on the social values of upper-class Victorian ladies. Meanwhile Mrs Jellyby, who allows her children to run wild while she pursues an obsession with African mission work, is a criticism of the growing role of Victorian women activists who pursued issues at a cost to their families. The death of Krook through spontaneous combustion (used as a cliff hanger at the end of a serial episode) was also topical. Many Victorians were sceptical about the phenomenon, which, in the nineteenth century, was attributed to alcohol consumption. In the Preface, Dickens refutes the sceptics by cataloguing the actual cases on which he based the incident.

Synopsis

A long-standing court case, Jarndyce and Jarndyce, which has dragged on for many years, involves, at the point that this novel is written, Mr John Jarndyce of Bleak House (formerly The Peaks), his wards Ada Clare and Richard Carstone, and Esther Summerson, whom he appoints as a companion to Ada. Many people have been ruined by this case. After meeting in London at the Court of Chancery, Ada, Richard and Esther all travel to Bleak House, where they are to live with Mr Jarndyce. Esther becomes the housekeeper; Richard and Ada fall in love. After much deliberation, Richard decides on a career in medicine and is placed in the care of a Chelsea surgeon. When this fails to interest him, he changes to law and then again to an army career. He gradually becomes engrossed in Jarndyce and Jarndyce, despite his guardian's pleas. Richard and Ada marry and have a child, but Richard becomes increasingly ill and dies just as Jarndyce and Jarndyce concludes, leaving them principal, but penniless, inheritors.

The story of Lord and Lady Dedlock of Chesney Wold runs alongside that of Richard and Ada. Lord Dedlock's callous lawyer, Mr Tulkinghorn, gradually uncovers evidence that Esther Summerson is the illegitimate daughter of Lady Dedlock and Captain Hawdon. He is murdered shortly after he threatens to tell Lord Dedlock what his wife has done. Lady Dedlock runs away and is later found dead.

Esther's story is also woven into the narrative. She is much loved by everyone and has many friends. After an attack of smallpox leaves her badly scarred, she agrees to marry John Jarndyce even though she loves someone else. She discovers who her mother is from Lady Dedlock herself, but keeps the information secret. Her story ends happily – after being released from her engagement to John Jarndyce, she marries the man she really loves, Doctor Allan Woodcourt, and lives contentedly with their children and Ada and her son.

Main characters

- Lady Honoria Dedlock, wife of Sir Leicester, in her forties
- Sir Leicester Dedlock, baronet, in his late sixties
- Mr Tulkinghorn, the Dedlocks' lawyer
- Esther Summerson, an orphan
- Mr William Guppy, a law clerk
- Mr John Jarndyce of Bleak House, Hertfordshire, Esther's guardian
- Ada Clare, Mr Jarndyce's orphaned ward
- Richard Carstone, Ada's distant cousin, also Mr Jarndyce's orphaned ward
- Nemo, a law writer, who is actually Captain Hawdon
- Mlle Hortense, Lady Dedlock's French maid
- Mr Woodcourt, a young doctor with whom Esther falls in love

Minor characters

- Miss Flite, an old lady with an interest in Jarndyce and Jarndyce, who spends every day in the Court of Chancery awaiting resolution of the case
- Miss Barbary, Esther's godmother and, according to the lawyer Mr Kenge, her aunt
- Mrs Rachael, Miss Barbary's servant, later Mrs Chadband
- Mr Kenge, a lawyer
- Miss Donny, proprietor of Greenleaf School, Reading
- Mrs Jellyby, a philanthropist with an interest in Africa
- Mr Krook, a landlord who owns a rag and bottle shop, brother to Mrs Smallweed
- Mr Harold Skimpole, who is befriended by Mr Jarndyce
- Mrs Rouncewell, the Chesney Wold housekeeper
- Rosa, the maid at Chesney Wold
- Watt Rouncewell, the housekeeper's grandson
- Mrs Pardiggle, the village philanthropist and her five young, but vicious sons
- Lawrence Boythorn, a friend of Mr Jarndyce and neighbour to Sir Leicester; once engaged to Miss Barbary

- Mr Snagsby of Peffer and Snagsby, law stationer, and his wife
- Guster, probably Augusta, servant to the Snagsbys, from a workhouse and cheap to employ as she suffers from fits
- Mr Bayham Badger, the surgeon who trains Richard Carstone
- Prince Turveydrop, a dancing teacher who marries the Jellybys' eldest child, Caddy
- The Smallweed family, grandparents, Judy and twin brother Bart (Bartholomew) Smallweed who works for Mr Guppy
- Tony Jobling, friend of Mr Guppy, who tries to find information about Nemo, also known as Mr Weevle
- Mr George, a soldier, formerly known as George Rouncewell
- Inspector Bucket, a detective
- Mr and Mrs Matthew Bagnet (a former soldier and colleague of Mr George) and their children Quebec, Malta and Woolwich
- Mrs Woodcourt, Allan Woodcourt's mother
- Volumnia Dedlock, one of Sir Leicester's many cousins

Settings

- Chancery, a court in London
- Chesney Wold, Lincolnshire, home of Lord and Lady Dedlock
- The London home of Lord and Lady Dedlock
- Greenleaf School, Reading
- Bleak House, St Albans, Hertfordshire
- Lincoln's Inn Fields, home and chambers of Mr Tulkinghorn
- The London homes of the Jellybys, the Smallweeds and the Bagnets
- Peffer and Snagsby, Mr Snagsby's shop, London
- Krook's rag and bottle shop, London
- The Turveydrops' dance school, London
- Mr George's fencing and shooting skills establishment, London
- The Lincolnshire country home of Mr Boythorn, adjacent to Chesney Wold

Themes

- Parents and children
- Death
- The law
- Secrets

Symbolism

- Caged birds
- Fog and darkness
- The East wind

Activities

Hooks, starters and pause points

Red tape * / **

Provide several lengths of red tape and allow pupils some time to discuss what its purpose might be. Then introduce the saying 'too much red tape' or 'cutting the red tape' and discuss what this might mean. During the nineteenth century, red tape was produced in Derbyshire tape mills in and around Wirksworth, just south of the Peak District, at the rate of 800 miles each week – enough, during Victorian times, to encompass the Earth. It is more correctly called 'legal tape' or, by defence lawyers, who still use it today, 'pink string'. It is now produced in Ashbourne in Derbyshire.

Dickens is credited with popularising the concept of red tape as representing too much bureaucracy, although red legal tape had been in use for hundreds of years before this. Whilst working as a Parliamentary reporter, David Copperfield describes 'Britannia ... skewered through and through with office-pens, and bound hand and foot with red tape', in other words, the government was so tied up in procedure and paperwork that it had become inefficient.

After discussing the above sayings, explain that *Bleak House* is about a law case called Jarndyce and Jarndyce, based on a real legal case which lasted for 53 years, ruining the lives of many people. The only people who got rich from both the real and fictional cases were the lawyers. A great deal of red tape would have been used in the course of Jarndyce and Jarndyce.

The lie detector * / ** / ***

Provide each pupil with a slip of paper on which they should write or draw three facts or statements about themselves. Two must be true and one must be false. Then, either in groups or as a whole class, ask pupils in turn to read out their three statements. Can the rest of the group/class spot the lie? Lead into the story, explaining that in the narrative there are lots of secrets and lies, which lead to people being very unhappy when these are exposed. Sometimes, telling one lie leads to another until a web of lies is formed.

Trapped * / **

Ask pupils to stand in a circle with arms linked. One person should stand in the middle of the circle; their aim is to escape. Every time the person in the middle tries to get underneath a pair of linked arms, the circle should close together to prevent them escaping. After several pupils have taken a turn at this game, discuss what it felt like to be trapped, even if it was only in a game. If anyone did escape, how did that feel? Explain that the book *Bleak House* tells the story of several people who are trapped. Dickens uses birds trapped in cages as a symbol of this. Just one character in the book has a bird which he allows to fly freely around when he is inside a house.

Chain reaction ** / ***

Use this activity as a lesson starter to review knowledge. Make a statement about the plot as a starting point. In turn, pupils have to add one sentence describing the next part of the plot until the review is complete. Chronology must be correct, so if part of the plot is missed by one pupil, the next person in the chain cannot backtrack. Review how much detail has been retained.

This activity can also be used as a plenary to review the learning in a lesson or as an instant assessment of learning at a particular point in a lesson. It gives the teacher insight into what needs to be revisited or reinforced and allows pupils to contribute to the direction of future learning by defining what gaps exist in their knowledge.

The final word ** / ***

This focuses attention on the detail of a given topic. For instance, you could ask pupils to list ten words which describe a character in the novel. Then the list must be reduced to five words and finally to the single, most significant word. Through shared discussion, decide on the quality of each person's or group's final word. What differences are there in the chosen words? Why are there these differences? This can be varied to focus on setting, plot or a particular feature of the novel. Pupils could be asked to choose 'the final word' using Dickens' language choices. It could also be used as an instant review of opinions.

The memory game ** / ***

Choose an image which relates either to the unit or an individual lesson. Allow pupils to view the image for thirty seconds and then to recall as much of the detail as possible. When everyone has contributed and a class list of content has been built, look again at the image. Was everything noticed? What was missed? What different impressions did the picture create? Why did each person remember something different? Reading image in detail is an important part of working within a visual medium so this activity is a good way to focus on visual information gathering.

Opposites ***

Start by providing a word. Pupils must provide the opposite. Continue until the activity is fluent. Then start to include words which reflect an aspect of the novel, for example truth/lies or rich/poor. Repeat the activity with pupils working in pairs. This could also be widened to include aspects of Victorian life which you wish to explore.

Magic dice ***

This can be used as a lesson starter or a plenary. Throw two dice and challenge pupils to give a corresponding number of facts and information about a given category. For instance, if you throw nine and you have been studying a particular setting, ask pupils to provide you with nine pieces of information about that setting. As a lesson starter, it reviews prior knowledge. As a plenary activity, it reinforces learning, allows the teacher to assess progress and encourages pupils to consolidate new knowledge which has been constructed during the lesson.

Body language ** / ***

Pupils walk around the room, pairing with the nearest person when asked to stop. Allow ten seconds (count down from ten to one) to create a scene which represents the emotion of happiness. Look at the scenes before asking pupils to resume walking around, again working with the nearest person when you say stop, to create a scene representing sadness during the ten-second countdown. After another pairing, create a scene to represent fear. After each scene, discuss how emotion was created without the use of words. Draw out that the emotions of happiness, sadness and fear concentrated on the use of facial expression to communicate.

Repeat the walking, pairing and countdown sequence to create paired scenes for master/servant, parent/child and friends. Discuss how these relationships can be represented without dialogue, exploring body language, posture, position and body proximity as a means of communicating to a viewer. Finally create scenes to represent ways of speaking, for example whispering, talking and shouting. How can body language intimate to a viewer how an actor is communicating?

Understanding character

Heard a rumour **

> **Objective**
> ● to use knowledge of a text to predict possible reasons for the actions of a character.

When Sir Leicester and Lady Dedlock married, she brought some property to the marriage which was part of Jarndyce and Jarndyce. Mr Tulkinghorn, as Sir Leicester's lawyer, is involved in the Chancery case and visits the Dedlocks shortly after they return to their London home from Chesney Wold, their country house in Lincolnshire. They are en route to Paris, about which Lady Dedlock is pleased as she has been very bored in the country. Sir Leicester has very little interest in the outcome of the case but will not take a view on the lengthy proceedings. He feels that to criticise the Court of Chancery would be to encourage opposition to the ruling class, of which he is a part. Mr Tulkinghorn places some papers about the case on a table near to Lady Dedlock, who is, as usual, very bored. Sir Leicester is so bored that he falls asleep whilst Mr Tulkinghorn is reading.

Share the narrative provided in text extract 3.1 *Lady Dedlock faints* – some prompt questions are also suggested. Allow pupils a few minutes to examine the extract and discuss in pairs why she might have fainted. Each person, acting in role as a servant in the house, then has to formulate their own reason for Lady Dedlock being taken ill. The whole class should circulate around the room, stopping to spread their rumour to every servant that they meet. After about five minutes, bring the class together and list some of the rumours. Which ones are plausible, based on knowledge of Lady Dedlock so far? Is she just ill, or is the author hinting at something darker? Retain rumours for discussion when the text is complete. How accurate or plausible were the explanations for the fainting episode?

Thought tunnel * / **

> **Objective**
> ● to interpret the actions of a character in the social context of a novel.

Use this activity at the point in the story when Lady Dedlock is about to run away from home. It could follow on from *Heard a rumour*. Review the facts so far:

● Lady Dedlock has secretly visited the place where Nemo lived and died (Chapter 16).
● Lady Dedlock has discovered from Mr Guppy that the baby whom she had always assumed to be dead was actually alive (Chapter 29).
● Mr Guppy also knows about the existence of letters which she and Esther's father, Captain Hawdon, the legal writer known as Nemo, exchanged and which Mr Guppy offers to sell her (Chapter 29).
● Mr Guppy then visits again to say that he has been unable to find the letters and does not know where they are or who has them.

- Lady Dedlock has met Esther at Chesney Wold and told Esther that she is her mother (Chapter 36).
- Mr Tulkinghorn has told her story anonymously at a gathering at Chesney Wold and Lady Dedlock is unsure about when he might tell Sir Leicester that his wife is the person in the centre of the story; Mr Tulkinghorn has told her that he intends to do so at some point (Chapters 40 and 41).
- Mr Tulkinghorn has been murdered and an anonymous letter falsely accuses Lady Dedlock of being the murderer (Chapter 55).
- Although at first Mr Tulkinghorn had persuaded her to remain with Sir Leicester for the sake of the family name, Lady Dedlock now thinks that her secret is so widely known that some-one must have told her husband. She decides to leave home.

Discuss why Lady Dedlock made this decision – in a Victorian context, it was shameful for a woman to have a child when she was unmarried. She had never told Sir Leicester about the child, believing her sister, who said that the baby had died at birth. What drives her decision – respect for Sir Leicester, shame, a desire to be with the man she really loved even if that meant death, or a wish to protect her daughter? What she could not know was that Sir Leicester loved her, would forgive her and wanted her to come home, regardless of the scandal that it might cause. She also could not have known that her former maid, Hortense, was the murderer. If she did stay, what might her hopes for the future be? It could help to hot seat Lady Dedlock before embarking on the thought tunnel.

Divide the class into two groups, lining up to face each other. Select one person to represent Lady Dedlock. The two lines act as her opposing thoughts when she is deciding what to do. Alternate between lines, with one line saying why it would be best to leave home and the other line speaking aloud her thoughts about staying with Sir Leicester. All comments should reflect the social context in which Lady Dedlock lived.

Finally, respond to this series of events by writing in role as Lady Dedlock. In the book, she leaves a letter for Sir Leicester apologising for what she has done. Write a different letter, explaining why she is leaving and the events of her life which have brought her to this point. Include as many references from elsewhere in the text as possible. Resource 3.1 (*Lady Dedlock's letter*) provides differentiated sample texts for shared reading, discussion and formulation of success criteria.

Who's who **

> **Objective**
> - to investigate how an author uses language to create character.

One of Dickens' greatest skills as a writer was in his creation of character. This activity exam-ines seven of the main characters in *Bleak House*, analysing how Dickens used language to create them.

Text extract 3.2 *Character profiles* contains information about the seven characters, Sir Leicester Dedlock, Lady Honoria Dedlock, Mr Tulkinghorn, Esther Summerson, Ada Clare, Richard Carstone and John Jarndyce. Read the extracts together, discussing and noting the meaning of any unknown words. Working in pairs, highlight key words in the text and discuss how these are used to convey character: for example, the following key words are used about Ada Clare – *golden, soft, bright, innocent, trusting* – compared with these key words for Mr

Tulkinghorn – *rusty, black, close, irresponsive.* How do these word choices immediately create an image? Is there any difference in the sound of the words?

Resource 3.2 is a template for a *Who's who* profile – resource 3.3 is an exemplar. Analyse the exemplar – the profile should demonstrate an understanding and interpretation of Dickens' language, not merely a repetition of it. When this is complete, evaluate the effectiveness of the profiles – how well has Dickens' meaning been inferred and deduced? As an extension activity, provide a sheet on which pupils can profile themselves, or a friend. They can use digital images of themselves or draw portraits. Evaluate the effectiveness and accuracy of word choices in conveying character and then bind the pages into a class *Who's who* book.

Understanding plot

*Murder most foul * / ***

Objective

● through shared discussion, to consider evidence and form evidence-based conclusions about an issue.

In addition to the social and legal commentary of *Bleak House*, the book is also a detective novel – possibly the creation and first example of the genre. The narrative is littered with clues which are brought together in this activity, which should be completed before revealing who the real murderer was. There are various suspects; resources 3.4 (*Murder most foul*) and 3.5 (*Murder most foul extension*) provide differentiated cards with the details of each suspect, including any motive for the murder.

Set the scene before handing out the cards. Mr Tulkinghorn is a lawyer for some very rich and influential people. When he is introduced at the outset, the reader is told that he has become rich from handling the marriage contracts and wills of the upper classes. Although seen at fashionable gatherings, he never imposes himself and only speaks if he is questioned. He is therefore very self-controlled and probably quite calculating. The reader is also told that he knows a great deal of confidential information about his clients, which he keeps entirely to himself. Very little is known about him – his offices are at Lincoln's Inn Fields. He appears to have some secrets of his own. 'Though a hard-grained man, close, dry and silent, he can enjoy old wine with the best. He has a priceless bin of port in some artful cellar under the Fields, which is one of his many secrets.'

After one particular visit to the Dedlocks with information about Jarndyce and Jarndyce, in which Lady Dedlock has an interest, he is surprised to see Lady Dedlock, who is normally very measured, faint when she observes the writing on a legal document. He pursues this and discovers Lady Dedlock's guilty secret – that she had a child with a Captain Hawdon before she met Sir Leicester and it is his writing which she recognised. She believed the child to be dead. Doing some detective work of his own, Mr Tulkinghorn discovers that the child was brought up by Lady Dedlock's sister, Miss Barbary, and she is alive, well and residing with John Jarndyce as Ada Clare's companion. There are also letters which Captain Hawdon and Lady Dedlock, then Honoria Barbary, exchanged which would prove her guilt. In the course of his detection, Mr Tulkinghorn upsets several people – he appears to have a web of knowledge which allows him to threaten or blackmail anyone who gets in his way.

Resource 3.6 announces the murder of Mr Tulkinghorn – print several copies of this and display them around the classroom for pupils to see as they come into school. At this point, do not engage in any discussion about it – leave pupils to discuss it amongst themselves. When you are ready to start the activity, move into role as Inspector Bucket, a detective officer; one prop is enough to move you from teacher to teacher in role. Ask pupils to work with you to solve the murder. The following facts are known:

- the murder was committed shortly before 10pm
- the victim had just returned home from a visit to Lady Dedlock
- a gunshot was heard
- a bottle of wine was opened but it was nearly full
- one glass was on the table with the bottle
- two candles had been lit but then extinguished quite soon afterwards.

Explain that at the point at which they have joined the murder enquiry, Mr George, a well-known local ex-soldier, has been arrested and charged with the murder; he is protesting his innocence and he has given you another line of enquiry to follow. You are by no means convinced of his guilt. Your assistants need to help you to decide if this is a wrongful arrest and, if it is, to find the real murderer.

Split the class into groups of detectives, giving one *Murder most foul* resource card to each group. Rotate cards every few minutes, after time has been given for group discussion and for notes about the suspect to be made. When this is complete, still working as teacher in role, compile an incident board. Is there conclusive evidence against any suspect? Through shared discussion of the available evidence, decide whether you should a) release Mr George and/or b) charge one of the other suspects with the murder.

Objective
- to write a chronological report using given information.

Using the evidence, notes and information from the group discussion, write a police incident report based on the actions of one of the suspects. Use evidence to justify points made and the decision to charge or not charge the character with the offence. Differentiated text samples are provided as resource 3.7 (*Police incident report form exemplar*). Review text structure, formal language and prior knowledge of chronological report writing to create appropriate success criteria before pupils embark on the independent task (resource 3.8 *Police incident report form template*).

Secrets and lies * / **

Objective
- to understand how behaviour choices can be governed by social expectation.

The word 'secret' appears more than 80 times in this narrative. As a result of these secrets, characters sometimes have to tell lies in order to keep their secret hidden. The first part of this activity examines the concept of secrets, lies and why we tell them, in the contemporary context of children's lives. Resource 3.9, *Secrets and lies*, contains a number of different scenarios. Working in groups, ask pupils to discuss each situation, deciding whether the outcome is good or bad. When the scenarios have been sorted into 'good' and 'bad' discuss what criteria were used to make the decision – this is usually intention. For example, is telling a 'white' lie always bad – we keep secrets that are intended as surprises so that we do not spoil the surprise. Can pupils read the intention behind each of the scenarios? This could be usefully contextualised as a circle time activity. People keep secrets and lie for a range of reasons – to keep themselves out of trouble, to protect others, to belong in a social group, to attract attention to themselves, to gain approval or to exert power over others. Can pupils sort the scenarios into these categories and add some suggestions of their own?

The second part of the activity looks at scenarios from the narrative. Resource 3.10 *Secrets and lies in Bleak House* outlines some of the secrets and the lengths that characters have to go to in order to cover them up. Can pupils read the intentions here? Why did the characters act in the ways that they did? What could they have done differently? Lady Dedlock had to keep her secret because of the rules of Victorian society. What would the equivalent be today?

Understanding setting

Fog * / **

> **Objectives**
> - to deepen understanding of literary devices through the interrogation of a text
> - to use language imaginatively to create atmosphere in a setting.

This activity is linked with *Great Expectations* to create a cross-textual plan exploring weather as a setting. The theme plan, available on the accompanying CD, is called *Mr Dickens forecasts fog.*

The opening of *Bleak House* is arguably one of the most powerful of any of Dickens' books. The rich imagery of the first two paragraphs is dominated by the use of anaphora, a device which Dickens uses in all of his novels. It is, quite simply, the repetition of a word or phrase for the sake of emphasis. As Dickens often read his stories aloud, the repetition would have had a significant effect on the listener. Using text extract 3.3 (*Fog*) read the opening paragraphs aloud. Ask pupils at the end of the reading which word stands out. Discuss why Dickens might have used this word so many times in just one paragraph. Read the second paragraph again and ask pupils to count how many times they hear the word 'fog'.

Talk about what it feels like to walk in thick fog, encouraging children to visualise the experience and choose descriptive vocabulary to talk about it. Introduce the concept of symbolism, discussing any symbols that children might be aware of, for example the colour red representing danger in a Western culture, a cross representing Christianity, Hedwig the snow-white owl representing the goodness of Harry Potter, the Tudor Rose representing the union of the families of Lancaster and York or the daemons representing their characters in Philip Pullman's trilogy *His Dark Materials* – pupils will be able to think of more examples. What might the fog described at the opening of *Bleak House* represent? How might fog relate to the ongoing lawsuit with its confusing documents and interminable legal exchanges? How relevant is it to use fog as a symbol of this confusion and why is it used at the opening of the narrative?

Then, provide pupils with copies of the text extract, reading it aloud as often as necessary. Ask them to work in detective teams to find examples of:

- alliteration
- simile
- personification

- varied sentence lengths
- contrast
- powerful verbs
- verbs used to describe the actions of the fog.

Through shared discussion, decide what effect this richness of language has on the reader or listener. For example, what is the effect of starting a book with the word 'London' or a paragraph with 'Fog everywhere'? How many different verbs are used to describe the way the fog moves? What is the effect of contrasting the black, sooty rain with snowflakes? How might it feel to stand above the fog and look down on it? (The modern equivalent would be flying above cloud). Conclude the discussion by deciding what overall effect these two paragraphs have on the reader or listener. What do readers expect to happen next? What sort of atmosphere has it created?

Next, ask pupils to choose another weather form which they have experienced, for example, sun. What sort of story could be introduced by using sunshine as a symbol? Practise writing some similes about the sun. To do this, brainstorm some characteristics of the sun – bright, shiny, hot, etc. Find an object which describes these characteristics (diamonds, fire) and create the simile, for example, 'the sun was like a fire'. Then improve the verb, so 'the sun shone like a fire'. If the simile describes a sunset, it could read 'the sun glowed like a fire', or for mid-day sun try 'the sun seared the earth like a ball of fire'. Encourage pupils to play around with words, trying different images. Finally, to create a powerful simile, add adjectives, for example, 'the setting sun glowed red like a dying fire' or 'the sun seared the earth like a ball of raging fire'. Alliteration adds to the power of the language. Read these similes aloud and discuss how effective they are in creating images in the mind of the listener.

Ask pupils to combine this language work into one paragraph, describing the effect of their chosen weather in the way that Dickens does in the opening of *Bleak House*. Read the completed paragraphs aloud and evaluate the effectiveness.

Houses and homes – the Jellybys * / **

Objectives
- to visualise a setting from an author's written description
- to use a visual stimulus to write a factual description of a known setting.

This activity is also repeated in the *Understanding setting* sections of *Great Expectations*, *David Copperfield* and *Hard Times* so that the theme can be studied either in one book or as a comparison of Victorian houses and homes across a range of texts. A theme plan, entitled *Houses and homes*, is available on the accompanying CD.

Dickens appealed to various senses when creating settings – sometimes he described smell in great detail and sometimes the visual sense was appealed to. The latter was the case when Dickens described the Jellybys' home. Mrs Jellyby typified many Victorian ladies who got involved in good causes – in this case, the fictitious African country of Borrioboola-Gha. Mr Kenge described her to Ada, Richard and Esther as devoted

> to an extensive variety of public subjects at various times and [she] is at present (until something else attracts her) devoted to the subject of Africa, with a view to the general cultivation of the coffee berry – AND the natives – and the happy settlement, on the banks of the African rivers, of our home population.

These ladies were often criticised for failing to care properly for their families and it is this aspect of the philanthropist that Dickens parodied in Mrs Jellyby – the chapter is titled 'Telescopic Philanthropy'. Her home was chaotic, her children were neglected and her husband was over-looked in the cause. Ada, Richard and Esther stayed at the home overnight, forming a friendship with Caddy, the frustrated eldest daughter who acted as Mrs Jellyby's secretary, before travel-ling from London to join Mr Jarndyce in St Albans.

Read text extract 3.4 (*The Jellybys' home*) aloud, asking pupils to visualise the scene as they listen. When you have finished reading, discuss what they can remember from their visualisa-tions. Make a list and consider how much detail Dickens gives his reader. Discuss the humour of the situation – curtains held together with a fork, good, but uncooked food and the cook leav-ing the pub at breakfast time. Could people really have lived in this way, or is Dickens using the literary technique of hyperbole, or exaggeration, to make a point?

As a response, ask pupils to write about a setting which they know well, such as their own home. The writing should appeal to the visual sense, so include as much detail as possible of what the writer can see, in order to paint a picture in the mind of the reader. As an extension challenge, pupils could experiment with using hyperbole. Then pair pupils and ask one pupil to draw the setting which their partner has described. How accurate are the pictures? The more detailed the description, the clearer the image should be. Pupils can ask questions while they are drawing in order to clarify detail. The writer should then add this extra information to their writing to increase the power of the description.

City and country * / **

> **Objective**
> ● to explore how setting can be used to portray issues which relate to social context.

Dickens was a social activist who commented regularly in newspaper articles about the living and working conditions of the poor. In Victorian London, it was quite possible for decaying slum buildings to be close to the homes of very wealthy people. The slums were inhabited by migrant workers, children and anyone who could pay rent and wanted to avoid the workhouse. In *Sketches by Boz*, published in 1836, Dickens wrote that the slums were

> Wretched houses with broken windows patched with rags and paper; every room let out to a different family, and in many instances to two or even three – filth everywhere – a gutter before the houses, and a drain behind – clothes drying, and slops emptying from the windows; men and women, in every variety of scanty and dirty apparel, lounging, scolding, drinking, smoking, squabbling, fighting, and swearing.

Read text extract 3.5 *City and country* which describes Tom-All-Alone's, the fictional slum in *Bleak House* where Jo the crossing boy lives. Ask pupils to list, or highlight on the text, the words which describe the slum. Then do the same with the description of the country estates of Mr Boythorn, and Lord and Lady Dedlock. Ask pupils to create two illustrations for the text of *Bleak House*, one of Tom-All-Alone's and one of the Dedlocks' country estate. How could colour be used to sharpen the contrast, for example pencil for the slums and watercolour for the country?

Compare the completed images. What have pupils learnt about the difference between city slums and country estates in Victorian times? Why has Dickens created these contrasts in the novel?

Whole text responses

Video diary room **

> **Objective**
> ● to reflect on the role of the protagonist in the course of a narrative.

Esther Summerson is the protagonist of this story. Her character profile (text extract 3.2 *Character profiles*) shows how shy and self-effacing she is. However, Dickens used her as a first-person narrator for considerable parts of the narrative, eventually bringing her story together with Lady Dedlock's strand of the narrative at the conclusion of the story. Because she is a first-person narrator, her reactions to situations are documented in the text. This activity examines these situations and uses text-based evidence to create a video diary response at each important stage of her story.

Divide pupils into eight groups. Give each group a section of Esther's story (resource 3.11 *Esther's video diary*). Older pupils can read the full chapter that their section relates to. Younger pupils can use the synopses provided, which contain some brief text extracts. Each group should prepare a video diary entry for their section. Hot seating Esther during the preparation for this could provide greater insight into her reactions. Alternatively, discussion questions are provided at the end of each section of the resource sheet.

Before filming the video diary, scripts will need to be prepared for each section. Because a video diary is improvisatory in nature, the script should be notes or prompt headlines rather than a written script which is read to camera. Pupils should talk in role as Esther and their videos should appear conversational in tone. If video cameras are not available, pupils could individually prepare a written diary page based on the section of Esther's narrative which they have studied. In this case, language would be structured but informal and might include sketches, pressed flowers and notes. People who keep diaries often record their thoughts and feelings about the day, rather than a chronological account of their actions – this should be reflected in pupils' writing.

This activity can be followed for any of the main characters in *Bleak House* by using the chapter outlines to locate relevant chapters in the novel.

Trapped in the web? **

> **Objective**
> ● to show understanding of plot structure and its effect on the behaviour of the central characters.

Miss Flite is an old lady in the novel who has spent so many years following Jarndyce and Jarndyce that her mind is now a confusion of reality with facts in the case and stories in the Bible. She still believes that the case will be resolved in her favour and that she will be able to solve all her financial problems. She keeps about twenty caged birds, larks, linnets and goldfinches, in her rented room at Krook's rag and bottle shop. She herself says, 'I began to keep the little creatures … with the intention of restoring them to liberty', but goes on to say that, 'They die in prison, though. Their lives, poor silly things, are so short in comparison with

Chancery proceedings that, one by one, the whole collection has died over and over again.' She then adds, 'I positively doubt sometimes, I do assure you, whether while matters are still unsettled, I may not one day be found lying stark and senseless here, as I have found so many birds!' There is a parallel here with the case itself, described at the outset of the narrative: 'The little defendant who was promised a new rocking horse when Jarndyce and Jarndyce should be settled has grown up, possessed himself of a real horse, and trotted away into the other world.' Miss Flite is afraid to let the birds out of the cages because of Krook's cat, Lady Jane, which she describes as being 'greedy for their lives'.

This is a perfect cameo symbol of the wider theme of the novel. Most of the characters are trapped in some way, either in unhappy relationships, by Jarndyce and Jarndyce or by secrets and lies. Even Esther Summerson has a caged bird which she takes with her when she moves from her aunt's home in Windsor to boarding school in Reading. Lady Jane is a symbol of the case itself, which has been responsible for the wasting of many lives. Only Mr Boythorn, a neighbour of Sir Leicester's in Hertfordshire, is free. He stands up to Sir Leicester's bullying and he is the only character who possesses an uncaged canary which flies freely and stays with him of its own free will. Introduce the narrative by explaining how the caged birds are a symbol of, or represent the position of, the characters in the story.

A web diagram is provided (resource 3.12 *Caught in the web template*) to plot the position of the main characters in relation to Jarndyce and Jarndyce as the story progresses. A completed exemplar (resource 3.13) is also provided for support or to prompt discussion.

Interactive PowerPoint presentation **

Objectives

- to communicate personal responses to a novel
- to reflect critically on a novel.

Using the interactive PowerPoint template provided as resource 3.14 (*Book review*) create a review under the headings Character, Plot, Settings and My Comments. It will provide a lasting record of your pupils' views of *Bleak House* and can be used as a study resource for future readers of the novel. Pages can be built by individual pupils or pairs, or a group could produce a complete PowerPoint working collaboratively.

Media studies

All of the following activities are based on the BBC television adaptation of *Bleak House*.

Roll the credits ** / ***

The opening credits are a very detailed collage of names, faces and objects. Watch the opening, running the DVD slowly. In addition to the names of the actors, list everything that can be seen – this may need several viewings. Can pupils find anything in addition to:

- a seal with the letter B
- a pair of scales
- an ink bottle and quill pen
- a lady's fan
- a red background

- a portrait of a soldier
- a bottle
- a medal
- a gun
- a lobster
- a lady's chatelaine
- white flowers
- a pile of legal documents tied with legal tape
- string.

What might all these objects mean? Do any of them have obvious connotations, for example, the scales representing justice and the white flowers representing truth and purity? Can any aspects of the story be predicted from these credits?

What might the tone of the film be?

The book or the film? ***

> **Objective**
> - to compare the effectiveness of literary devices with media devices in creating the setting of a novel.

Read *The opening*, text extract 3.6, from the opening of the novel and consider these questions through shared discussion:

- What literary devices does Dickens use to create an effective setting?
- What atmosphere does Dickens create?
- How do you react as a reader?

Then watch the opening of the film version. Through shared discussion, decide:

- Is the same atmosphere created?
- If so, how does the director of the film achieve this?
- If not, what atmosphere is created and why?
- What devices are used in filming which cannot be used when writing?

Which version of the opening of *Bleak House* is the more effective? What are the advantages and disadvantages of a film?

Foreshadowing ***

> **Objective**
> - to explore the effect of foreshadowing on the plot and the media devices used to achieve it.

Discuss foreshadowing and how it can be used as a literary device. Discuss known examples of foreshadowing in books that pupils have read. Then watch episode 2, asking pupils to find examples of foreshadowing as they view the episode. For example, what is the significance of the bundle of letters which Krook finds in Nemo's chest and to which he returns later in the episode? Consider Lady Dedlock's reaction to the note from Mr Tulkinghorn – what questions does it raise in the mind of the viewer? What was Mr Tulkinghorn suggesting at the conclusion of his conversation with Lady Dedlock? What might be the significance of Esther's conversation with Mr Woodcourt in the mind of John Jarndyce and how is this communicated to the viewer? What techniques were used to provoke these questions? Remember to consider sound, body language and the contrast of light and darkness, together with other media devices. Find and discuss as many examples of foreshadowing in the episode as possible.

Through discussion, review the meaning of the terms 'connotation' and 'denotation'. How are they used to foreshadow events in this episode? What is the effect of foreshadowing on the viewer? Conclude with a discussion about how foreshadowing as a literary or media device affects the plot.

Mr Skimpole's conversation ***

> **Objective**
> ● to consider the effect of foreshadowing on plot.

Read text extract 3.7 (*Mr Skimpole's conversation*) and discuss its meaning. What is he trying to persuade Esther, Richard and Ada to believe about him? Then consider the conversation which Skimpole has with Richard in episode 2 scene 2 of the TV version whilst they are walking in the garden. Apart from the obvious differences of setting and participants, what is the difference in the intention of the two conversations? What is Skimpole foreshadowing in the film conversation? What seeds is he sowing in Richard's mind about the possibilities of his future and the intentions of John Jarndyce? How is the viewer's understanding of his character enhanced? What effect might this have on the plot? In the book, he appears to be as innocent as a child until much later in the narrative. Why?

Exploring emotion ***

> **Objective**
> ● to explore how emotion is transferred from the page to the screen.

Read the conversation which Esther and Ada have one evening (text extract 3.8 *Exploring emotion*). Pair pupils to make a list of the emotions contained in the scene and compile one definitive list through shared discussion. What literary devices has Dickens used to communicate the emotions of the scene to the reader? How might this translate to the screen?

View the same scene at the opening of episode 3, with muted sound for the first viewing. How are the emotions translated to the screen? Watch the scene again with sound. What extra elements does this add? Have all the emotions listed in the narrative version been translated into the media version? How have media devices been used to communicate? Which of the scenes do you think is more effective?

Jo visits Mr Tulkinghorn ***

> **Objective**
> ● to explore the effectiveness of the plot structure when a novel is adapted for television.

When adapting a novel for film or television, the screenwriter has to consider how to use the original plot structure. In this activity, a scene from the DVD is compared with Dickens' narrative to explore how the structure of one scene in the novel is translated to the screen. Watch the opening scene of episode 5 when Jo visits Mr Tulkinghorn's chambers. Then read the narrative version (text extract 3.9 *Jo visits Mr Tulkinghorn*) before discussing these questions, together with any other questions that pupils formulate whilst watching the film and reading the text:

● What are the similarities and differences?
● What is the reader left asking about the lady in the veil?
● What does the viewer become aware of about the lady?
● How can film provide knowledge which a written narrative cannot?
● What might Dickens' intentions have been in leaving the reader in ignorance?
● How might the screen information affect your prediction about outcomes?
● Which version of this scene is more effective and why?

Mise-en-scène ***

> **Objective**
> ● to understand the term *mise-en-scène* and be able to use it in the correct context.

Explain the term *mise-en-scène* and its context within a moving image study. It is an expression used to describe the design of a film, including the set design, props, actors, lighting, costume and the use of space – in other words, what a director sees through the camera. An example of a *mise-en-scène* analysis can be found at http://www.cod.edu/peopl/faculty/pruter/film/manhattan.htm. Discuss how the analysis is structured and how the director uses all available resources to communicate. Then create a class *mise-en-scène*, choosing a suitable still from each of the following:

● The Court scene, episode 1 scene 1
● Nemo bumping into Esther outside court, episode 1 scene 1
● Miss Flite feeding her birds, episode 1 scene 4
● The burial of Nemo, episode 2 scene 2.

Next, provide pupils with text extract 3.10 *Miss Flite's birds* which describes one of the scenes analysed above. Compare the text with the *mise-en-scène* which the class created. What are the differences? Choose another still from the film and ask pupils to work independently to write a *mise-en-scène* analysis.

Character quest ***

> **Objective**
> ● to consider how language is used to describe characters.

Resource 3.18 (*Character quest one*) contains descriptions of several characters who are introduced in the first fourteen chapters of the book. Read the statements aloud one at a time and ask pupils to attempt to work out after hearing each statement which character is being described. More information is given with each statement. Which piece of information made it possible to identify each character? What prior knowledge of the characters did pupils recall to help with identification?

Continue by discussing how these characters have been adapted in the film version. What else can be added to moving image that is not easily conveyed in a novel? How are the characters rounded and given greater depth in the film version? How accurate are the interpretations to Dickens' own descriptions?

The above activity can be extended with text extract 3.11 (*Character quest two*) which contains Dickens' profiles of the main characters of the novel, John Jarndyce, Lady Dedlock, William Guppy, Mr Krook and Harold Skimpole. In what ways are the film and narrative descriptions of the main characters similar? In what ways do they differ? What can be achieved through film which cannot be achieved through writing? Do pupils interpret the characters in the same way as the film's director? If they were directing the film, what would they do differently?

The Ghost's Walk at Chesney Wold ***

> **Objective**
> ● to demonstrate knowledge and understanding of media techniques by creating a short film.

The outcome from this activity is to make a film about the Ghost's Walk. Read text extract 3.12 (*The Ghost's Walk at Chesney Wold*), which explains the Dedlock family myth. The Ghost's Walk is mentioned for the first time in Chapter 2 and a further twenty times in the course of the novel. Why is it referred to so many times? Brainstorm initial ideas for a film, then divide pupils into groups to storyboard their films. Drawing on prior knowledge of adaptation for film, does the complete narrative need to be used, or just part of it? What media devices could be used? What might be foreshadowed by the closing of the scene, which implies that it is Lady Dedlock who is most aware of the sound whenever it rains, even though she has tried to drown it out?

Complete this section of the preparation by using a spot check in which each group provides one idea which will be used in the film – this could be about the use of the camera, music, actors' body language or use of light and colour to create atmosphere. Use this as an opportunity for formative assessment of pupils' understanding and prior knowledge of media strategies.

Continue by pairing groups to share plans so far. Identify the techniques which will be used. Discuss any techniques that are missing and brainstorm ideas about how to include them. In the course of the film making, ask pupils to discuss how their films reflect Dickens' description of the Ghost's Walk and the atmosphere he created. At least three quotations should be included which support decisions that have been made about the film content.

When complete, watch each film and analyse it using the following criteria:

- media devices
- foreshadowing
- connation and denotation
- body language
- social and historical context
- plot structure and shot structure
- colour
- lighting
- creation of atmosphere
- characterisation
- camera shots.

Which devices were easiest to incorporate? Which were most effective? Which were the hardest or required the most planning?

Camera shots ***

Objective

- to examine how important camera work is to the success of a scene.

To produce the most effective films possible, pupils need to develop understanding of the use of the camera. These websites provide a wealth of information to which pupils should refer throughout this unit in order to develop their knowledge and expertise.

- http://www.bbc.co.uk/drama/shakespeare/60secondshakespeare/directing_videos.shtml
- http://www.bbc.co.uk/videonation/contribute/tips/what_you_film/interesting_shots/index.shtml
- http://www.youtube.com/watch?v=TJ7SRLHw02o

Commercial break ***

Objective

- to use known media devices to create an advertisement.

Using Windows Movie Maker or iMovie, create a 60-second television advertisement about *Bleak House*. Pupils can use any combination of stills from film or other pictures, interviews with actors and critics or reviews, and actors' comments, to create their advertisement. Through shared discussion, determine what needs to be communicated. What is the purpose of an advertisement? How can media devices achieve this? Evaluate each advertisement for effectiveness of communication, persuasiveness and use of media devices.

⦾ Linked reading

Victorian Servants: A Very Peculiar History: Fiona Macdonald, Book House.
The Lottie Project: Jacqueline Wilson and Nick Sharratt, Yearling.

The Ruby in the Smoke: Philip Pullman, Scholastic.

The Stranger in the North: Philip Pullman, Scholastic.

Avoid Being a Victorian Servant: Fiona Macdonald and David Antram, Book House.

You Wouldn't Want to be a Victorian Servant: A Thankless Job You'd Rather Not Have: Fiona Macdonald, David Antram and David Salariya, Children's Press.

Hunted Down: The Detective Stories of Charles Dickens: Peter Owen Ltd.

Britten and Brulightly: Hannah Berry, Jonathan Cape.

The Necropolis Railway: Andrew Martin, Faber and Faber.

4 *David Copperfield*

Overview

Context and social background

David Copperfield is, in part, autobiographical. It is a *Bildungsroman* (literally, a growth and development novel), a genre in which the central character grows to maturity in the course of the narrative, often finding answers to significant questions and becoming socially successful by the completion of the story. Usually the protagonist suffers some event which causes a separation from their family – in David Copperfield's case, the event which led to him being sent to boarding school. From this point, David is largely alone as he deals with the issues he faces. The novel ends with the protagonist reflecting on his journey through life to success. Because of his naivety and immaturity throughout much of the novel, he is a good example of an unreliable narrator. As with many of Dickens' novels, it was first published in twenty instalments, with the final two instalments sold as a double issue. It was then published as a complete novel in 1850.

Although this book is not a vehicle for social comment in the same way as *Oliver Twist*, it does contain some social observation – the social climbing of Uriah Heep and Little Emily, both of which end in disaster, and the fact that whilst Mr Spenlow was alive, David was too inferior to marry Dora, but following her father's death, the match was considered very suitable. Class issues are also observed – James Steerforth is deferred to by the masters at school, and his mother does not consider Emily worthy of consideration or sympathy, even when her son ruins Emily's life.

Emigration to Australia was also reaching unprecedented numbers at the time that this novel was written. The 1851 census showed that there were nearly half a million single women in England. This was attributed to the mass migration of young men in search of a more prosperous life, particularly following the 1851 Gold Rush. In order to redress the gender imbalance that this created, single women were offered free passage to Australia on any of the twice-weekly sailings from London and Plymouth. Many women left in search of a social mobility that was denied to them in England.

Blunderstone, the place of David's birth and early life, is actually a village in Suffolk called Blundeston. The website http://www.blundeston.org.uk/ contains pictures of The Rookery, the setting for David's early life, the church where he fell off of the pew and The Plough Inn, from which the carrier Barkis started his journeys.

Synopsis

Writing in the first person, David Copperfield introduces his family in the opening chapter, including his father, who died six months before David was born; his timid mother Clara, a young orphaned governess with whom his father had fallen in love despite being twice her age; and Betsey Trotwood Copperfield, a formidable great-aunt who had once been married but who had separated from her husband and reverted to her maiden name. Aunt Betsey unexpectedly visits Mrs Copperfield, but leaves the house just after David is born, disappointed that the baby had not been a girl.

Mrs Copperfield meets Mr Edward Murdstone – Peggotty (the housekeeper) and Mrs Copperfield disagree about him. David is taken on holiday to Peggotty's family houseboat in Yarmouth for two weeks, returning to find that much has changed; his mother has married Mr Murdstone, a large, angry, black dog has taken up residence in the garden and his room has been moved elsewhere in the house. Soon Miss Jane Murdstone, Edward's sister, moves in and takes over the running of the house. After six months, in which David becomes increasingly scared of the Murdstones as they supervise the education which his mother is giving him, Mr Murdstone canes David as a punishment for not learning his lessons well enough. David responds by biting him. After several days locked in his room, he is sent away to school. Arriving during school holidays, he is required to wear a placard saying, 'Take care of him. He bites.'

David meets Traddles and Steerforth (the senior boy) and is drawn into the general admiration of Steerforth. David introduces him to the Peggottys when they visit him at school. During his second term, David is summoned home following the deaths of his mother and half-brother. Peggotty is dismissed by the Murdstones and marries Mr Barkis, the carter. David is then sent to work for Mr Quinion, washing bottles at Murdstone and Grinby's in London, and he lodges with the impecunious Wilkins Micawber. When the Micawbers move, David runs away to find his Aunt Betsey, who adopts him and renames him Trotwood. He is sent to school in Canterbury, lodging with her lawyer, Mr Wickfield. He spends several happy years here, before moving to London to train in law with Spenlow and Jorkins.

Following the death of Barkis, Emily (Peggotty's niece) runs away with Steerforth and the depth of his treachery becomes apparent to David. Aunt Betsey moves to London when she is financially ruined and David works as a secretary to Dr Strong in addition to his law training in order to earn more money. He becomes engaged to Dora Spenlow; her father is furious when he finds out. But after her father's death, her maiden aunts agree to the marriage. Dora turns out to be a hopeless housekeeper. Her health deteriorates after the stillbirth of their first child, whilst David's writing career starts to flourish.

Meanwhile, Mr Micawber starts working for Uriah Heep, who has taken control of Mr Wickfield and created himself a partner in the business, also intending to marry Mr Wickfield's daughter, Agnes. Eventually, Mr Micawber is able to unravel Heep's false accounting and Heep is forced to return the money he has stolen. Aunt Betsey is no longer bankrupt. Dora continues to get weaker and dies, followed shortly after by Peggotty's nephew, Ham, attempting to rescue Steerforth from a shipwreck. Steerforth is also killed. The Micawbers, Mr Peggotty and Emily emigrate to Australia. After travelling in Europe for three years after the death of Dora, David returns home and marries Agnes.

Main characters

- Clara Copperfied, widow and mother to David
- Betsey Trotwood Copperfield, great-aunt to David
- Clara Peggotty, the housekeeper
- Edward Murdstone, stepfather to David
- Jane Murdstone, Edward's sister
- Ham Peggotty, Emily Peggotty, orphaned nephew and niece to Peggotty
- Dan Peggotty, brother to Peggotty, Uncle to Ham and Emily
- Mrs Gummidge, widow who lives with the Peggotty family in their houseboat
- Mr Creakle, the proprietor of Salem House School
- Tommy Traddles, a school friend
- James Steerforth, senior pupil at Salem House
- The Micawber family; Wilkins, Emma and their four children

- Mr Richard Babley, or Mr Dick
- Mr Wickfield, Aunt Betsey's widowed lawyer
- Agnes, his daughter
- Uriah Heep, the clerk
- Mr Spenlow, the widowed lawyer to whom David is articled
- Dora Spenlow, his daughter and David's first wife

Minor characters

- Mr Chillip, doctor who attended David's birth
- Barkis, the carter
- Mr Quinion and Mr Passnidge, business associates of Mr Murdstone
- Mr Mell, a master at Salem House
- Mr Omer, a draper and haberdasher
- Dr Strong, the school principal
- Annie Strong, his young wife
- Mr Jack Maldon, Mrs Strong's cousin
- Mrs Markleham (the Old Soldier), Mrs Strong's mother
- Mrs Steerforth, James' mother
- Rosa Dartle, her companion
- Littimer, the Steerforths' servant
- Mrs Crupp, landlady
- Julia Mills, friend of Dora Spenlow
- Misses Lavinia and Clarissa Spenlow, maiden aunts to Dora

Settings

- Blunderstone, David's childhood home
- The Peggottys' house boat in Yarmouth
- Salem School, run by Mr Creakle
- The home of Betsey Trotwood, Dover
- Canterbury, the school run by Dr Strong and the home of Mr Wickfield and Agnes
- Mr Spenlow's home, London

Themes

- Families
- Love
- Power and weakness
- Trust and loyalty

Symbolism

- The sea
- Angels
- The crocodile book

Activities

Hooks, starters and pause points

*Special books * / ***

Introduce a special book which you have – this could be one from your own childhood, or one which you value at present. Talk about why you value it, when you read it, what memories you associate with it and perhaps whether you have a favourite place to sit and read. Ask pupils to do the same and share with a partner, group or class why they have chosen their special book. Without comment at this point, read the following three amended extracts, telling pupils that they have been written by a boy called David at three different stages of his life. Discuss the similarities in his experience of a special book with their own – attached memories, feeling safe and enjoying the company of the person reading the book.

Extract 1

Peggotty and I were sitting one night by the fire. I had been reading to Peggotty about crocodiles. She had a cloudy impression, after I had done, that they were a sort of vegetable. I was tired of reading and dead sleepy but having leave, as a treat, to sit up until my mother came home from spending the evening at a neighbour's, I would rather have died than have gone to bed. 'Let me hear some more about the Crockindills,' said Peggotty, who was not quite right in the name yet. So we returned to those monsters and we left their eggs in the sand for the sun to hatch, and we ran away from them, and we went into the water after them. We had exhausted the crocodiles and begun with the alligators when the garden bell rang. We went out to the door and there was my mother.

Extract 2

When we had had our tea and lit the candles, I read Peggotty a chapter out of the Crocodile Book, in remembrance of old times – she took it out of her pocket: I don't know whether she had kept it there ever since – and we talked about school and my friends. We were very happy; and that evening will never pass out of my memory.

Extract 3

And now my written story ends. I see myself, journeying along the road of life. I see my children and my friends around me. There is something bulky in Peggotty's pocket – it is the Crocodile Book, which is in a rather worn condition by now, with several of the pages torn and stitched across but which Peggotty shows to my children as a precious relic. I find it very curious to see my own childhood face looking up at me from the Crocodile Book.

Then introduce *David Copperfield*, explaining that although the book was written by Charles Dickens over 160 years ago, some aspects of the central character's life are the same as theirs today.

*For sale! * / ***

Collect a range of estate agents' leaflets and ask pupils to collect pages of house sale and rental advertisements from local newspapers. In groups, explore the leaflets and advertisements – what makes them attractive? When people are searching for a home, how do they decide where to live? List the reasons. How do estate agents both provide information and advertise? Do pupils think that people in the past have used the same criteria to decide where to live?

Ask pupils to bring images of their own homes into school, with information about why their parents chose to live there, whether their home meets all the needs of the family and what they like most about their home. Do pupils have their own bedrooms? Where is their private space? Does their home look different from others in the area, or are there lots of homes that look similar?

Explain that Charles Dickens wrote detailed descriptions of the homes of several of his characters and together you are going to examine some of them, to understand how Dickens used language to describe settings and also to compare some Victorian homes with their own homes.

Guess the picture * / **

Collect some photos of people as babies – this could be the children in your class, yourself as a baby, famous people or other members of staff. Share these with pupils and ask them to try to guess to whom the photos belong. When you have finished guessing and revealed who the owners of the images are, introduce the story of David Copperfield. Explain that the book is autobiographical – it is written in the first person and the narrator writes his own life story, beginning with his own birth. Read the opening chapter, or extracts appropriate to the age of those listening.

School days * / **

Provide pupils with nib pens and small bottles of ink with which to experiment. Ask them to write the alphabet – this is particularly challenging when joining letters. You could also provide slates and chalk as these were more commonly used in the classroom, pen and ink being reserved for writing on paper.

For more information, go to http://www.bbc.co.uk/schools/primaryhistory/victorian_britain/ and click on Victorian schools. This site is worth exploring – there are brief video clips about the school log book and the Victorian school day together with a wealth of facts and other information. Schools were not free until 1891, although all areas had to provide a primary school, run by the School Board, by 1880. Until then, poor children did not go to school at all as most of them had to work from a very young age. Wealthy children were educated at home by a governess, so only about half of Victorian children actually went to school at all.

Show your pupils a copy of *David Copperfield* and explain that it was written by Charles Dickens over 160 years ago and together you are going to explore some aspects of the main character's school life.

Who am I? ** / ***

Write the name of a famous person or character from a film or a book on a sticky note, ensuring that there are enough to stick one on the back of each pupil. They then have to ask each other questions in order to find out who the character is on their sticky note. The only banned question is 'Who am I?' Encourage the use of exploratory questions such as 'Am I a book or film character?' and 'Am I famous for doing something good or something bad?' When all pupils have worked out their character, discuss the questions which were asked. What kinds of questions were the most useful? Which ones did not give any useful information? How did the questioning move from general questions to very specific ones? What do you need to know about someone to know who they are?

Showing respect ***

David Copperfield lost two members of his family while he was still very young. He was also widowed after his wife lost their first child. Death following childbirth was common and the child mortality rate was high. Every society has its own ways of showing respect to the dead. Resource sheet 4.1 (*Showing respect*) has some facts about mourning in Victorian England. Read them together, discussing why each action might have been valued by those in mourning and how it differs from our modern practices.

New kid on the block ** / ***

There were occasions in the novel when David had to start a new life. On one of these occasions, he started at a new school. He had missed a lot of his education and was behind other boys. His first experience of school life had not been positive, so he would have had a range of thoughts going through his mind. This is a common experience with today's pupils, who will all have started a new school at some stage in their lives.

Ask pupils to think about how we present ourselves when we are in a new situation. What do we want people who do not know us to find out about us? Use an 'If I could start again I would' activity in which each pupil completes the sentence with a statement about themselves which they would like others to know. Then, working in groups, ask pupils to attempt this again, talking in role as David.

Friendship circle ** / ***

A key theme of the novel is the loyalty of friendship. Although David loses his mother when he is still young and his stepfather is cruel, he forms friendships at the first school which he attends which last throughout his life. Ask pupils to draw a friendship circle, showing the key relationships and friendships in their lives. Chose one relationship and one friendship that they feel have changed them or affected them most and write a sentence explaining why and how they did so. This should be retained if pupils are writing an autobiography.

Ball drop ** / ***

Stand pupils in a circle. Using a tennis ball, throw it to one person, who must throw it on to someone else. This continues until everyone has caught the ball. Pupils should fold their arms once they have caught it. The second time around, each person must give one piece of information about a given topic before throwing the ball on. This could be a particular character, part of the plot, the social background of the novel or a general recall of information about anything to do with the book, its background or context. If anyone drops the ball, they must think of two pieces of information. As an additional challenge, try a third round, in which each person must recall someone else's fact before they throw the ball to them. This could be used to start a lesson or as a pause point for formative assessment for both teacher and pupils.

Rites of passage ***

Each culture and society has its own rites of passage – times when a child or young person is separated from their normal environment and moves to another phase of their lives. Young Masai men in Kenya and Tanzania have to hunt and kill a fully grown male lion with a spear to prove their worth as warriors. In Japan, all young men who have come of age during the previous year celebrate as part of a national day each January, whilst young Aboriginal men have to survive in the Australian outback alone for six months as their rite of passage into adult life.

What rites of passage do we observe in our culture and how do we celebrate them? List birth, starting school, leaving home, family deaths, eighteenth birthday, graduating, starting work and marriage as some examples. Discuss at what age these rites of passage occur in our modern society. Using David Copperfield as an example, consider how this varied for Victorian children and young people.

Growing pains ***

Life for Victorian children and teenagers was very different from life for today's young people, regardless of class. Resource 4.2 (*Growing pains*) encourages pupils to reflect on these differences to deepen understanding of the background to the novel. Discuss answers when the sheet is completed. What conclusions can be drawn about life for children and young people in Victorian England? Can anyone think of a reason why it might have been better to grow up in the nineteenth century?

Dreams and aspirations ***

Use resource 4.3 (*Dreams and aspirations*) to consider how life plans for Victorian people were affected by social structure and values. Although the restrictions of class are no longer a social barrier to progress, what factors in our modern society affect social mobility or limit choices? Can dreams and aspirations be achieved any more effectively today than in Victorian times?

Understanding character

Most wanted * / **

Objective
- to examine how an author makes word choices to create a character type.

Some of the characters in *David Copperfield* are bad people. How did Dickens convey this? Was it just in their actions, or did he use words in other ways to create visual images in the minds of his readers? Text extract 4.1 (*Mr Murdstone*) contains information about one of those characters. The text extract is compiled from across the narrative, arranged and briefly linked where necessary. Pupils can evaluate Dickens' own language in deciding both what makes this character bad and how the reader knows this.

Read the text extract and highlight any words which communicate information about the character, including his name. Through shared discussion, decide how word choices portray character. Then, using both this information and the key points from the text extract sheet, create a MOST WANTED poster for Mr Murdstone – a template is provided as resource 4.4 (*Most wanted*). When possible, use Dickens' own words on the poster. Evaluate how effectively the posters communicate the character as it is portrayed by Dickens.

Family values * / **

Objective
- to deepen understanding of characters' feelings through inference.

Relationships within families form stark contrasts in the narrative – the cold, superior relationship of Mrs Steerforth with her indulged son, Clara Copperfield's warm, loving relationship with

David and the harshness of her second marriage, and the chaotic, noisy and supportive relationships within the Micawber family. Another close family in the book is the Peggotty family. This is comprised of Mr Dan Peggotty and his sister, Clara Peggotty – David's nurse and the Copperfield's housekeeper until Mrs Copperfield dies. Mr Peggotty also cares for his orphaned nephew, Ham, and niece, Emily, and Mrs Gummidge, the widow of a fellow fisherman who has died.

Using the samples in text extract 4.2 (*The Peggotty family*), highlight key words. Then, through shared discussion, decide which key words should be added to resource 4.5 (*The Peggotty family diagram*), which shows the interaction of the different members of the extended Peggotty family. Pupils can also add words of their own, either known facts about the characters or inferences from the given text.

Model the writing of a magazine article titled 'Meet the Peggottys'. Discuss what readers would want to know – who the family members are, what they do, how they feel about each other and how they care for and support each other, even when things go wrong. A text sample for modelling is provided as resource 4.6 (*Meet the Peggottys*). Pupils could also repeat this for their own families and then compare Dickens' narrative with their own – has anything changed, or do families still get on, fall out and sort things out?

Two to follow **

Objective

● to demonstrate empathy with characters.

Twitter encourages its users to follow other people's tweets by tagging them. There are recommendations of 'Who to follow' based on the user's interests. In studying the character of David Copperfield's friends, there are suggestions for just two to follow – his old school friend, Traddles, and his impecunious friend, Wilkins Micawber.

Two to follow (text extract 4.3) contains text extracts and story points about each of the characters – you can choose to study one, or both. In pairs, pupils should work in role, one as a magazine interviewer and one as a chosen character. The interviewer poses a question, which must be answered by the character using no more than 140 characters – this includes spaces and all punctuation. This poses a significant challenge for the writer – what will be included? What can be left out? What can be abbreviated but still allow the reader to make sense of the word? For example:

Interviewer: What are you doing right now?
Mr Micawber: My difficulties are coming to a crisis. I fear I am about to be arrested. Until smthng turns up (of which I am confident) I have nthng!

If conducted in a chat room, this activity would possess genuine spontaneity. The content of the chat could be edited and refined to produce a focused interview. Alternatively, the interview could be produced in writing, with the outcomes from each pair of pupils formatted as a series of magazine interviews. Sharing of these through a wiki created for the purpose would allow collaborative evaluation and comment as the interviews were posted. There are two advantages to this – the activity would have the immediacy of online journalism and pupils could make collaborative responses without having to wait their turn to speak in a whole class shared discussion. The teacher is also able to comment whilst the writing is taking place.

Text comparisons ***

> **Objective**
> ● to examine how characters are affected by their life circumstances.

Compare David's descriptions of his new school in Chapter 6 with his descriptions of Yarmouth in Chapter 3. How does Dickens use language to communicate David's very different reactions to very different circumstances? Write a paragraph comparing his emotions, using quotations where appropriate to support observations.

Compare Dickens' presentation of the people and surroundings in Chapter 13 with those of David's home and the Murdstones in Chapters 1 and 2. Examine the language which Dickens uses to describe the characters. How does he convey that Mr Murdstone is a bully or that Aunt Betsey is kind, although stern? Write a paragraph explaining how Dickens' use of language creates a contrast between the two situations. How does Dickens signify the importance of the characters in each chapter?

Friendship matters ***

> **Objective**
> ● to explore how language can be used to describe the character of a person.

Using text extract 4.4 (*Friendship matters*) compare the characters of Traddles and Steerforth. What can the reader see about Steerforth that David, as a young and innocent child, is blind to? Why does David feel this way about Steerforth? On the evidence available so far, which person is likely to be the most reliable friend? Complete a dual *Role on the wall* (*Understanding character: Great Expectations*) sheet for both boys. Include quotations where appropriate.

Based on the information Dickens has given us, what predictions could be made about the future of each of these characters? For each prediction, give the quotation that it is based upon. David re-establishes contact with both Traddles and Steerforth after they all grow up. Conclude by discussing which person is more likely to make a valued and loyal friend to David in adult life. Challenge pupils to provide evidence from the text to support their viewpoint.

In the director's chair: family tensions ** / ***

> **Objective**
> ● to interrogate a text in order to deepen understanding of how language is used to communicate character.

Imagine that you have been asked to direct an episode of a serial titled 'David Copperfield: My Story'. You will be directing the episode which focuses on family tension and suffering. Read Chapters 8 and 9, then create a script for one of the following scenes involving David:

● returning home to find a new baby, with everything he knows having changed
● the tensions of living with his step family
● the death of his mother and the aftermath.

Scripts should be annotated to show where characters stand, body language, facial expression and posture. Focus on the emotions that each character, particularly David, experiences. How would you direct the camera in order to communicate the emotion that the scene is portraying?

View the directed scenes, then complete the activity by discussing how Dickens' language was used when making decisions. Write a paragraph about Dickens' use of language to communicate emotion. Include quotations and evidence from the text to support decisions.

Understanding plot

Here I am! * / **

Objectives

- to explore the opening section of an autobiography
- to consider how a writer uses humour to engage the reader.

David Copperfield is an autobiography, so this activity examines Dickens' account of the central character's birth and early life. Many of the details of the book shadow Dickens' own life, so it is assumed that it is, at least in part, also Dickens' autobiography. He closes the preface to the 1869 edition of the book with the words, 'Of all my books, I like this the best … like many fond parents, I have in my heart of hearts a favourite child and his name is David Copperfield.'

Either through shared reading or reading aloud, discuss text extract 4.5 *Here I am!* Then explain that pupils are going to find out how the writer uses words to make the reader laugh. To do this, use the *Here I am! Mime cards* (resource 4.7). Mime is an art form which communicates without words. This means that body language and facial expressions are the only means of communication. You can introduce mime and find demonstration warm-ups at http://chartier.rainbowwings.org/. These ideas can then be taken into the preparation of the mimes, during which groups can discuss what they are doing. Performances, however, must be completely silent. Stop regularly to review the work of individual groups and to allow collaborative discussion about developing each mime.

Each performance needs to be filmed – this will be greatly enhanced if the person operating the camera is cineliterate. To explore this, read the cineliteracy section in Chapter 1 of this book. Video each performance, view the videos and discuss how each group met the challenge of communicating the humour of the situation without using any words. Evaluate how effectively this was done. End by returning to Dickens' text and re-reading it.

- How have the mimes deepened pupils' understanding of humour?
- How effective is this as an opening to an autobiography?
- How has humour engaged the reader?

The journey of life * / **

Objective

- to understand how a plot is constructed.

Resource 4.8 (*The journey of life*) takes the form of a board game in two differentiated versions. To play, each pair or group will need one die and each player will need one counter. This will not only help pupils to grasp the flow of the complete plot, but will also facilitate shared discussion. Use these questions and ask pupils to formulate some of their own:

- Why did the author introduce Aunt Betsey at the beginning of the book and then suddenly remove her from the story until much later?
- Which is your favourite character? Why?
- Who has the greatest influence on David's life?
- How do the ups and downs of David's life reflect our own lives?
- What good decisions did David make during his life?
- Which situations in his life did he have no control over?
- What bad things happened to him? What did he do about them?
- Can we learn anything by reading a book which was written over 160 years ago? If so, what can we learn?

A blank version of the game is included for pupils to make an autobiographical game of their own lives so far.

Couples in love ***

> **Objective**
> - to compare Dickens' presentation of relationships and consider what this shows readers about Victorian society.

There are two couples in *David Copperfield* whose relationships are woven into the narrative. Compare and contrast the relationship of Steerforth and Emily with that of David and Dora. The first of these is detailed in Chapters 31, 32 and 46, while David and Dora's relationship is described in Chapters 26, 33, 37 and 41. In what ways do these relationships reflect the morals of Victorian society and the middle-class view of marriage represented by David and Dora, compared with Emily's views on social climbing and Steerforth's upper-class view of the value of working-class women? Why would Steerforth not have treated a lady in the same way that he treated Emily? What do these chapters tell the reader about the characters of the four people involved? Note ideas using resource 4.9 (*Couples in love comparison*).

Harry Potter

> **Objective**
> - to consider similarities in autobiographical structure between a Victorian and a contemporary text.

Many of the issues faced by David Copperfield are common to the issues of our modern society. As an autobiographical series of novels, the Harry Potter series has several parallels with *David Copperfield*. Some comparisons are suggested below. Challenge pupils who know the Harry Potter texts to find other parallels.

- Compare David Copperfield's experience in starting school (Chapters 6 and 7) with *Harry Potter and the Philosopher's Stone* when Harry is talking to Ron on the train and Hermione is looking for the toad (*Harry Potter and the Philosopher's Stone*, Chapter 6 – The Journey from

Platform 9 and 3/4). Focus on the emotions and experiences of trying to make new friends and settle in.

- Compare David's treatment and feelings when he runs away (Chapter 13) to those of Harry Potter when Aunt Marge comes to visit and Harry runs away (*Harry Potter and the Prisoner of Azkaban*, Chapter 2 – Aunt Marge's Visit). Focus on the language and the emotions that the situation evokes in a) the characters and b) the readers.
- Compare Chapter 18 to Harry Potter falling in love (*Harry Potter and the Order of the Phoenix*, Chapter 21 – The Eye of the Snake). Discuss falling in love for the first time – what are the common experiences to both David and Harry?
- Compare Chapter 19 to Harry Potter's interview with Umbridge (*Harry Potter and the Order of the Phoenix*, Chapter 29 – Careers Advice). Show direct links between the two books via quotations to show that the emotions involved for David Copperfield are still relevant today.
- Compare the ending of *David Copperfield* with that of the *Harry Potter* series (*Harry Potter and the Deathly Hallows* epilogue, 19 Years Later). Are they similar in any way? Widen the comparison to include your knowledge of both stories. Has much changed in terms of story-telling since Dickens was writing?

Understanding setting

*Houses and homes * / ***

Objectives
- to explore Victorian houses and homes as described by one author
- to compare and contrast Victorian and contemporary houses and homes.

This activity is also repeated in the *Understanding setting* sections of *Bleak House*, *Great Expectations* and *Hard Times* so that the theme of houses and homes can be studied either in one book, or as a comparison of Victorian houses and homes across a range of texts. A theme plan, entitled *Houses and homes*, is available on the accompanying CD.

Houses and homes, text extract 4.6, describes Blunderstone Rookery, the house where David Copperfield was born and spent the early years of his life, and the Peggottys' houseboat, where the Peggotty family lived and where David often stayed as a child and young man. Read the extract which describes Blunderstone Rookery to the whole class, challenging listeners to visualise the house as you read. Next, use these questions to discuss what pupils have heard and visualised.

- Why did the chickens seem big to David?
- Can pupils recall any situations where something or someone has seemed big, only to discover as they grow up that this is not the case – it's a matter of relative size?
- Why do you think he dreamt about the geese?
- Why did he mention the store room? What smells particularly stayed in his memory?
- Do pupils have any cupboards or areas of their homes that they were afraid of as a small child?
- Are there any smells which are particular to their homes?
- Why did the house have two parlours?
- The author describes the kitchen and two parlours. Which part of the house is not described? Why?

- What was David's back garden like?
- Which two senses does Dickens appeal to in the reader?

After shared discussion, read the text extract again, encouraging visualisation. Then explain that pupils are to produce an estate agent's leaflet about Blunderstone Rookery, using the information in the text extract. Provide text samples for highlighting key words and facts. Encourage the use of Dickens' vocabulary where possible.

This can be repeated with the Peggottys' house boat, using the following questions:

- What surrounded the house boat? There are clues to answer this question at the beginning and the end of the extract.
- Why do you think that someone had turned a boat into a home?
- What did the inside of the house boat look like?
- Why was the bed so small?
- What did people in the boat sit on?
- Why do you think that David was so excited about the house boat?

An estate agent's sheet is available as resource 4.10 (*For sale*). When this is complete, return to the original text to evaluate the accuracy of the description.

To extend this activity further, ask pupils to photograph or sketch their own homes and either:

- create an estate agent's leaflet for their home

or:

- write a description of their home, using descriptive vocabulary.

Encourage the inclusion of what the writer can see, hear and smell to create a detailed description.

School days * / **

> **Objectives**
> - through shared discussion, to interrogate a text describing two contrasting school settings
> - to compare these settings with the reader's current experience
> - to write persuasively, using knowledge and information from group and class discussions.

This activity is also repeated in the *Understanding setting* section of *Hard Times* so that the theme of school days can be studied either in one book or as a comparison of Victorian schools across a range of texts. A theme plan entitled *School days* is available on the accompanying CD.

David attended two schools: Salem House, as a boarder, where he was sent after biting Mr Murdstone, and Doctor Strong's school in Canterbury after he was adopted by his Aunt Betsey. Read the extracts and compare the two experiences – for teachers, the extracts are provided as *School days* (text extract 4.7). For pupils, the text is divided into manageable sections, with discussion questions about the text following each section (resource 4.11 *School days discussion cards*). There are also questions to encourage pupils to make comparisons with their own school buildings and daily experience.

Divide the class into nine groups, providing each group with one card. Allow time for discussion and comparison, before rotating the cards between groups. Repeat this two or three times.

Then, through shared class discussion, compile a list of features for Mr Creakle and his school, Doctor Strong and his school and your own school. Encourage pupils to refer to the text to explain and justify their views about David Copperfield's schools. Also encourage precise vocabulary choices when describing their own school. Discussion points and the word bank can be noted on resource 4.12 *School days discussion grid*, as not all pupils will have discussed all of the cards.

Using the outcome of the discussion, write either:

● an advertising poster for one of the schools which Dickens describes and an advertising poster for your own school, contrasting the two posters

or:

● a persuasive letter to a prospective parent, explaining the virtues of the school.

In either case, encourage pupils to use some of Dickens' own vocabulary where relevant. Resource 4.13 (*Persuasive letter*) suggests the angle which Mr Creakle may have taken in trying to persuade parents that their child would thrive in his school. A simpler text using Doctor Strong's school is also available for younger pupils.

*Journeys and transport * / ***

> **Objective**
> ● to understand how a writer from a different time presents experiences.

This theme is also explored in the *Understanding plot* section of *Hard Times* so this can be studied within one book, or across both texts to gain a wider picture of Victorian transport. A theme plan entitled *Transport* is available on the accompanying CD.

David Copperfield reflects some of the travelling that Victorian people did and the ways that they moved around. In the first part of the nineteenth century, road travel was undertaken in a range of carriages, depending on the length of the journey and the wealth of the traveller. Continental travel involved sailing ships, then later steam ships, across the English Channel, whilst emigration to other countries, such as Australia, involved a three-month sea voyage in a sailing ship.

By the time the novel was published, many English towns and industrial centres were accessible by train – a mail train had certainly superseded the mail coach to Yarmouth when *David Copperfield* was written. However, Dickens has set the narrative in a time prior to the railway, when travel was still by coach. Characters in the novel travel regularly from Yarmouth to London, and London to Dover and Canterbury. At the end of the book, David also travels around Europe, following a well-travelled route through the Alps to Switzerland.

Stagecoach journeys, so called because the journey was undertaken in stages, were the principal way that early Victorians moved from one town to another. At one point, four stagecoaches a day made the journey from Yarmouth to London, one of which is described in the book. The first part of the journey was by cart, from Blunderstone to Yarmouth. Dickens describes David arriving at the coaching inn to find the coach without horses – stops at inns allowed for passengers to eat whilst the horses were changed. Coaching inns fulfilled the same purpose for the Victorian traveller as motorway service stations do for the modern traveller. Roads were also owned by turnpike trusts, so brief stops had to be made to pay turnpike charges – similar to toll roads and toll bridges today, although much more frequent.

To investigate coach travel, divide pupils into small teams – about six children per team works well. A picture of a stagecoach can be found at www.nationaltrust.org.uk/main/w-arlington-carriage-list.pdf. Print the picture and cover up all but a few centimetres of it. Ask the first child in each team to come to the front of the room, study what they can see for one minute, then return to their groups and draw what they can remember. With the next child in each group, reveal a few more centimetres of the picture for them to draw. Repeat this either until all children have drawn part of the picture or until the images are complete. Compare the finished pictures – how closely do they resemble the original picture? Discuss what details of the coach were noted during the close observation activity.

Then read text extract 4.8 (*Transport*) in which David describes his journey from home to London. Referring to the picture, decide where David would have sat. How comfortable would this have been for an overnight journey lasting seventeen hours? Using Google Maps® or a road map of Suffolk, work out David's journey. Many coaching routes followed old Roman roads and the Yarmouth to London route was no exception. The modern A12 follows a similar route, although the modern road bypasses the towns and villages where coaching inns were used. Can pupils find Darsham and Saxmundham on the map? These are just two of the stops which the stagecoach made. How far was the stagecoach journey? How fast did the stagecoach travel if it took seventeen hours to cover the distance? How much quicker would it be today, and how many different ways can the journey be made?

Ask pupils to talk with a partner about a journey which they have made. This could be by car, train, coach, bus or plane. In the way that Dickens describes what David saw and the people with whom he travelled, pupils should describe fellow travellers and what they could see as they travelled. After this verbal rehearsal, ask them to map their journey in pictures to show how they travelled, whom they were with and what they saw en route. Brainstorm vocabulary and note it on the map. Finally, use all of this information to write a travel entry for a magazine, complete with illustrations or digital images if any are available. Bind all the contributions together to create a class travel magazine.

How is travelling a different experience today from that of David Copperfield's time? Consider mode of transport, speed, comfort and safety. In what ways is it similar? Have people really changed, or just the way they move around?

Whole text responses

Chat room **

> **Objective**
> ● to respond to a character with empathy and write reflectively in role.

As pupils read, or listen to, the story, ask them to write reflectively in role as David Copperfield. If your school has a VLE, use the Chat Room for this. Alternatively, www.primarypad.com could be used, an online collaborative writing pad which allows up to 15 people to be involved. Working in pairs, review a scene from the narrative which involves the protagonist. Decide whether the communication is a text or chat – this will depend on the amount of information which is being relayed. Decide with whom David would be communicating, then step into role and write. Some suggestions for suitable scenes are made below. Over the course of the study of the novel, this activity would build into a response to many of the key events in the text.

- Visiting the Peggottys' house boat for the first time
- Salem House School
- Working at Murdstone and Grinby
- Life with Aunt Betsey and returning to school
- Steerforth's betrayal
- Meeting Dora
- Getting married
- The death of Ham
- Emily's return
- The Peggottys and Micawbers leaving for Australia
- Communicating with Agnes whilst travelling around Europe
- Communicating with the Peggottys and the Micawbers.

This is me! * / **

> **Objective**
> - to understand autobiography as a form of chronological report which needs to inform and entertain the reader.

Ask pupils to collect pictures of themselves at key points in their lives: birth, birthdays, with family members, starting school, enjoying hobbies, success and humorous incidents. Interview at least two family members about birth and early life (either using resource 4.14 *This is me!* or linking the interview to the photographs collected). Think about how to start the autobiography. Read these starting lines; what makes them effective? How is the reader's attention grabbed? Ask pupils to think about some good starting lines for their own autobiography – rehearse some examples with a partner and choose the most effective.

- 'I must confess, I was born at a very early age.' (Groucho Marx)
- 'Whether I shall turn out to be the hero of my own life, or whether that station will be held by anybody else, these pages must show.' (*David Copperfield*)
- 'To begin my life with the beginning of my life, I record that I was born on a Friday at twelve o'clock at night.' (*David Copperfield*)
- 'My father's name being Pirrip and my first name being Philip, my infant tongue could say nothing longer or clearer than Pip. So I called myself Pip.' (*Great Expectations*, paraphrased)

Using resource 4.15 (*This is me planning sheet*), plan the autobiography. Remember to include in each paragraph as much information as possible from birth until today. How might humour play a part in an autobiography? How would this affect the reader? Decide how to structure the text and then write the autobiography. This could be:

- a formal, written presentation
- a calendar with one image and associated writing for each month
- a PowerPoint presentation with a sound commentary and photographs which have been annotated on www.superlame.com
- an e-book using Microsoft Photo Story 3
- an autobiography created at www.OurStory.com
- a download of the free Open University app Our Story (available for iPhone, iPad and iPod Touch from itunes.apple.com), which allows users to upload images and add text and sound.

This would be particularly valuable for reluctant readers or children who speak English as an additional language or with limited English.

Autobiography ***

> **Objective**
> ● to demonstrate understanding of the genre of autobiography.

For older pupils, a response could more closely match the structure of Dickens' novel. As an ongoing task during the study of the novel, prepare and write an autobiography in instalments:

Part 1: The birth story

After reading David Copperfield's description of his birth, write the first instalment of an autobiography.

Part 2: My family

Create a map of your town. Label places of interest such as friends' houses, places you used to visit in your childhood, your school, etc. Then, around pictures of family members, introduce the characteristics, behaviours and actions that define your family to your readers. Reflect on how you are defined by the people around you.

Part 3: My first holiday

Pupils should consider how the people around them and the change of scenery when they were on holiday made them feel and influenced their choices about what they did.

Part 4: My first day at school

Pupils should express their emotions through their writing, recalling memories and impressions as they had them at the time, rather than a teenage interpretation of their memories. Think about how Dickens described David's emotions on his first day at school.

Part 5: New friends

After studying David's friendships with Steerforth and Traddles, pupils should describe at least two of the friends that they have made at school.

Part 6: Tough times

Thinking about emotive language, pupils should write about a time in their past that they have found particularly challenging.

Part 7: The important people and places in my life

Think about the use of language to describe people accurately. Reflect on Dickens' use of language to create contrasts for the reader.

Part 8: Big school

Pupils should write about their time (so far) at secondary school. What do they hope to achieve during their time at school? What will make them successful? What emotions does Dickens describe that are common to everyone?

Part 9: My rite of passage

After considering rites of passage in contemporary life, write about one important rite of passage encountered so far. Reflect on the tone of the writing. Are there any good or bad angels, as defined by Dickens, who have influence?

Part 10: My dreams and aspirations

Consider David Copperfield's dreams for his life. Write about your own.

Part 11: My worries about the future

Reflect on the issues which worried David Copperfield and his wife as they embarked on married life. Think about how Dickens made language choices to communicate this to the reader.

   The autobiography can be pictorial in the form of a collage, or in text form, as appropriate to individual pupils.

○○○ **Linked reading**

Jackie Daydream: Jacqueline Wilson and Nick Sharratt, Doubleday.
Dear Mr Morpingo: Geoff Fox, Wizard Books.
I am David: Ann Holm, Heinemann.
Long Walk to Freedom: Nelson Mandela, Macmillan Children's Books.
Harry Potter and the Philosopher's Stone: J.K. Rowling, Bloomsbury.
Harry Potter and the Chamber of Secrets: J.K. Rowling, Bloomsbury.
Harry Potter and the Prisoner of Azkaban: J.K. Rowling, Bloomsbury.
Harry Potter and the Goblet of Fire: J.K. Rowling, Bloomsbury.
Harry Potter and the Order of the Phoenix: J.K. Rowling, Bloomsbury.
Harry Potter and the Half-Blood Prince: J.K. Rowling, Bloomsbury.
Harry Potter and the Deathly Hallows: J.K. Rowling, Bloomsbury.
Private Peaceful: Michael Morpurgo, Harper Collins.
Lord of the Flies: William Golding, Faber and Faber.

5 *Great Expectations*

Overview

Context and social background

Great Expectations was published in serial form between 1860 and 1861, in the magazine *All the Year Round*, which Dickens founded and owned. It succeeded *Household Words*, in which *Hard Times* was published. Commenced in 1859, the magazine continued in print for some 20 years after Dickens' death, being produced by his son, Charles. The novel *A Tale of Two Cities* was also published in *All the Year Round*.

Similarly to *Hard Times*, the novel is free of subplots and minor characters as it was published in weekly, not monthly, episodes. It is set in Kent, an area which Dickens loved and knew well. At the start of the novel in 1812 Pip, the protagonist, is about seven years old. He grows up in a village on the Kent marshes – Cooling is thought to be its inspiration, as the churchyard of St James church in Cooling contains some lozenge-shaped gravestones similar to those described by Pip. The model for Miss Havisham's house, named Satis House in the novel after a house in Cooling, still stands and is called Restoration House – a brief video of it can be viewed at www.digitaldickens.com. Moored on the Medway were prison hulks, ships waiting to take convicted criminals to Australia. Dickens would have been familiar with these from his life in Chatham, when he would have been able to see the moored hulks.

As with *David Copperfield*, this is a *Bildungsroman*, autobiographically tracing the growth and development of Pip, an apprentice blacksmith who wants to become a gentleman. It is a comment on the desire for upward social mobility and the class divide of Victorian society. Love, horror, crime and poverty were also popular genres in Victorian novels and Dickens includes all of these strands in a novel which was written primarily for financial reasons. Just a year before *Great Expectations* was published, Samuel Smiles, a Scottish author, published a book entitled *Self Help*, which reflected the Victorian view that one's lot in life could be improved by hard work and determination. Smiles' book developed from a speech made many years earlier and published as *The Education of the Working Classes*. Dickens firmly believed that education was a route to self-improvement.

Synopsis

Pip, the central character in the novel, is an orphan who is being brought up by his sister, Mrs Joe, and her husband, Joe, the village blacksmith. She has a sharp tongue and Pip often feels humiliated. One evening, whilst visiting the graves of his parents and brothers, Pip is stopped by a convict who threatens to kill him if he does not provide food and a file to remove his leg irons. Pip steals the things and takes them onto the marshes the following morning, returning home to celebrate Christmas with his family. During the evening, Pip and Joe join a group of soldiers who find the convict and return him to the prison hulk moored on the river.

One evening, Mrs Joe returns from a shopping trip with Joe's Uncle Pumblechook to say that the wealthy Miss Havisham requires a child to visit her house and Pip has been suggested. The experience is painful, as Pip is mocked by Estella, Miss Havisham's adopted daughter, for his rough clothes and manner of speech. He feels ashamed of his background. However, he continues to visit until, one day, Miss Havisham asks Joe to visit with Pip. She gives him 25 guineas and tells Joe to indenture Pip as an apprentice blacksmith. Pip is told not to visit again, although he does go once more on his birthday, only to find that Estella has been sent to school abroad.

In the pub one night, a stranger who identifies himself as a lawyer tells Pip that an anonymous benefactor wishes to pay for his education and help him to become a gentleman, so Pip leaves Kent for a new life in London. He lodges with the Pocket family and lives so expansively as a gentleman that he eventually runs into debt. He grows too proud to have much contact with his family until he discovers that his benefactor is actually the convict, Magwitch, not, as he had assumed, Miss Havisham. As circumstances start to spin out of control, Pip realises the true value of Herbert Pocket's friendship and the worth of his family. Facing financial ruin following the death of Magwitch, he moves abroad, working to pay off his debts and earn the respect of those people who love him most.

In the original story, Pip meets Estella many years later after her cruel marriage ends but he no longer cares for her. In the published version of the novel, they promise never to be parted even though Pip has grown beyond his desire to be socially acceptable to Estella. The debate continues about which ending is more consistent with Pip's mature character and the tone of the narrative.

Main characters

- Pip, or Philip Pirrip, son of Philip and Georgiana, both deceased
- Joe Gargery, blacksmith, who takes care of Pip
- Mrs Joe Gargery, Pip's sister
- Mr Pumblechook, Joe's uncle
- Abel Magwitch, also known as Provis, a convict
- Miss Havisham
- Estella, Miss Havisham's adopted daughter
- Biddy, Mr Wopsle's relation, who helps to run a school and cares for Mrs Joe
- Herbert Pocket, relative of Miss Havisham and friend to Pip
- Mr Jaggers, a lawyer acting for Pip's anonymous benefactor

Minor characters

- Mr Wopsle, the church clerk
- Mr Hubble the wheelwright and Mrs Hubble
- Miss Sarah Pocket, a relative of Miss Havisham
- Dolge Orlick, a blacksmith journeyman
- Mr Wemmick, Mr Jaggers' clerk
- The Aged, Mr Wemmick's father
- Miss Skiffins, friend, and later wife, of Mr Wimmick
- Mr Skiffins, her brother
- Bentley Drummle and Startop, two other lodgers with Mr Pocket

Settings

- A graveyard
- The home and forge of Joe Gargery
- The Kent marshes
- Satis House, the home of Miss Havisham
- London: Barnard's Inn, the Temple, Hammersmith, Walworth, Richmond

Themes

- Dreams
- Class
- Self-improvement
- Friendship
- Pride

Symbolism

- Prisoners
- Gatekeepers
- Fog
- Darkness

Activities

Hooks, starters and pause points

The time of my life * / **

Ask pupils to choose the six most significant events in their life so far – something in their family or something which has happened to them personally. Events might be positive or negative. Encourage pupils to share either in pairs, groups or as a whole class. Do pupils have any thoughts about how these events have affected them or their families?

Explain that *Great Expectations* is about a boy called Philip Pirrip. The book is an autobiography and opens with the line, 'My father's name being Pirrip, and my Christian name Philip, my infant tongue could make of both names nothing longer than Pip. So I called myself Pip, and came to be called Pip.' Practise saying Philip Pirrip – even for older children it is quite hard to say! Pip has already suffered some very significant life events when the novel opens, as he is an orphan. He has no memory of his parents or the five brothers who have also died. He has just one sister left, who is grown up and married to the local blacksmith. They care for him. How have these events in Pip's life affected him? What might have happened to him if he had not had a sister to look after him?

Tug of war * / **

A tug of war is a very appropriate game to introduce one of the themes of *Great Expectations*. After a few games, discuss with pupils the science involved. It is based on two people or two teams pulling in opposite directions. A well-balanced game can last some time, pulling first one way, then the other. Where forces are unbalanced, one person or team quickly wins. What other examples can pupils think of where tension is created, but balance can be maintained, through applying opposing forces?

Pulling in opposite directions can apply to relationships, too, and this is a central theme of the novel. Tension exists in several of the book's relationships and also in actions – at one point, Pip steals some food from home to feed a starving convict. This creates a moral tension as he tries to balance the guilt about stealing with the good of caring for someone in trouble. Some examples of these tensions and how they are resolved will be explored.

Mirrors * / **

Pair pupils for this game. One person leads and their partner follows. Change the leader regularly. The aim is for the follower to copy everything that the leader does, as if they were a reflection in a mirror. After several changes of partner, watch some pairs at work. Discuss how the aim of the game is achieved – the follower has to watch and copy every move carefully in order to create an accurate reflection.

Pip, the protagonist in this novel, plays a real-life game of mirrors. He is dissatisfied with his life and wants to be a gentleman when he grows up, rather than a blacksmith. When he is given the opportunity, he does so by watching and copying carefully until he changes himself into a gentleman.

Mum's the word * / **

Ask each pupil to draw a picture of their mum and write around it some words which describe her and how they feel about her. How do mothers make us feel about ourselves? Share some of the words and discuss what they tell the listener about the writer's view of the person being described. Can we tell what the relationship between two people is by the words which are chosen to describe it? Two characters in *Great Expectations*, Pip and Estella, are both orphans and are brought up by very different adopted mothers. One of the activities will explore the words that Dickens used to describe them.

Book covers ** / ***

Find ten different cover designs for *Great Expectations*. With pupils working in pairs, ask them to read the images in detail, including background/foreground, salience, perspective and colour. The visual grammar section of Chapter 1 of this book provides information about reading images. What might the book be about? What can be predicted from the covers about genre, character, plot and setting? Through shared discussion and the contribution of each pair of pupils, decide what the story and settings might be. Retain this information to return to during the study of the book, testing predictions and ideas for accuracy.

I don't believe it! ***

Resource sheet 5.1 (*I don't believe it!*) contains some facts and information about the Victorian penal system. For each statement, pupils should decide if they think this statement is correct (all of the statements are accurate and factual). Discuss how fair the justice system was – was everyone given access to equal treatment? Discuss how this differs from our justice system today. Is our society more or less fair? How have our values changed? Is poverty a reason to turn to crime in our modern society?

Book people ** / ***

This starting activity encourages pupils to think about characterisation in books which are currently popular. Provide four or five character statements about a chosen book character and ask pupils to work out who the character is – this could also be led by individual pupils or used as a group activity. Then focus on one or two characters from *Great Expectations*. For example, the character statements for Magwitch could be:

- he was very considerate of people's feelings when they were kind to him
- he had made some really bad decisions in his life

- he wanted to help someone achieve their dream even though his life was ruined
- he was a victim of his circumstances from birth.

Can you tell what it is yet? ** / ***

This activity sharpens visual literacy skills whilst also developing prediction skills. It can be used as a hook into a unit or an individual lesson starter. Choose an image which relates to the unit or lesson and slowly reveal the image. At each stage of the reveal, discuss the detail which can be seen and use this to predict what the whole image might communicate. Revisit earlier predictions as more of the image is revealed – how accurate were the predictions? How were they amended as more of the image became available?

Through shared discussion, establish what information can be gathered from reading images and why they are used in books, newspapers and websites. Refer to the section on visual grammar in Chapter 1 of this book to enhance understanding of how information is communicated through image.

Class sort ***

Review knowledge about Victorian social structure and class definition, then categorise the people on resource sheet 5.2 (*Class sort*) according to class. Some suggested questions for discussion could include:

- What were the constraints on each class?
- Were men and women similarly constrained or were there equal opportunities to change class?
- How far could a person move?
- Was there downward as well as upward social mobility?
- How do we define class today?
- What are the constraints on upward mobility in modern society?

Is it something I said? ** / ***

What assessments do we make about people based on the way they speak? How do we categorise them? Does regional accent shape our view of people when we first meet them? Do we create stereotypes? Can we make assumptions about the level to which a person has been educated based on the way they talk? What does the way we use language today denote – social, ethnic or age groups?

In Victorian society, people could be grouped by class according to how they spoke and how they pronounced words. Pip is very ashamed of how Joe speaks – read the conversation in text extract 5.1 (*Is it something I said?*) and compare how Joe speaks with how Miss Havisham structures her language. Rephrase some of Joe's comments to show how Pip would like Joe's pronunciation and use of language to become more refined in order for him to sound like a gentleman. Discuss how Dickens uses language to portray social status.

Class change ***

Using resource 5.3 (*Class change*) list on the left of the diagram everything which has been learnt so far that would categorise Pip as working class. For each criterion, draw a line to the right-hand side and describe what would need to happen in order for Pip to move to a higher class. How high can he move? What are the constraints acting on him becoming upper class?

Money, money, money ** / ***

Discuss the significance of money in our lives. What song lyrics and TV soap plot lines can pupils think of in which money is the centre? Ask pupils to work in groups, and then share as a class, completing the statement 'If money were no object …'. Are there any common dreams? Would the realisation of dreams based on money necessarily make us happier?

In Victorian society, money denoted class. The concept of a middle class was becoming established, as merchants and self-made men began to dominate the economy of the country and the upper class defined itself by birth, inherited wealth and the right to govern. But poverty and lack of education equated to working class, so money denoted status in a way that is less clear in our society.

What difference might money make to Pip? What would he need to change to move to another class? Do pupils predict that he will make these changes?

Witnesses ** / ***

Choose any film clip, such as a topical news item, to show pupils. After viewing the clip, pair pupils and ask them to each describe to their partner what they witnessed. Then choose pupils to report to the class not on what they saw, but what their partner reported. Discuss how these recounts differ.

Through shared discussion, decide why people might witness things in different ways. It could depend on physical location, where the witness was looking at the time and the way that memories are recalled. For example, some people will recall sounds, some will recall a particular colour and some will recall atmosphere and emotional reaction. But we also filter what we see and assess it according to our personal viewpoint.

Conclude by discussing how Pip might view people in a higher class than himself. Would other characters, for example Joe, have a similar view? What affects our view of society and our place in it?

Recap jigsaw ** / ***

This can be used to start a lesson or check knowledge about a character or the plot. Give pupils a sheet of plain paper on which they should write several facts about the given subject. Text can be entered horizontally, vertically or diagonally, or in blocks scattered around the sheet. Next, draw some simple shapes over the writing and cut it up to create a jigsaw. Exchange with another pupil and make the jigsaw.

Multiple choice ***

Working in pairs, ask pupils to write a multiple choice question about a character, with three or four predictions about what could happen to that character as the novel progresses. For example, a question could read:

Does Miss Havisham:

- become kinder as she gets older
- persuade Estella to marry Pip
- die
- find the man she once loved and marry him?

Pupils should exchange questions and decide on the most suitable prediction based on knowledge about the story so far.

Your starter for three ***

Use this as a starting activity when you want to review prior knowledge about particular characters. Pupils must work out which character you are describing, but only three statements are provided. Give more specific information with each statement, so for Estella, you might say:

● this character is female (this could be any one of Mrs Joe, Biddy, Miss Havisham or Estella)
● she was rich, but very lonely (Miss Havisham or Estella)
● she was educated abroad (Estella).

Pupils could also do this in groups or with one pupil leading the class, as it focuses attention not only on the detail of a character but also on common features between characters which are useful when sequencing the questions. Structured thinking is needed in order not to give too much information away too quickly.

If pupils lead this activity, it provides the teacher with an opportunity to informally assess both the depth at which an individual pupil is engaging with characterisation, and also the development of thinking skills.

Friendship matters ***

This can be used to start a lesson, but it also gives insight into how much understanding each pupil has of Dickens' characterisation. It could be used towards the end of a unit of work, to assess knowledge and understanding.

Provide some scenarios and for each one, ask pupils to decide what Pip, Estella, Miss Havisham and Magwitch might do. For example, what would each of these characters do if:

● a friend wanted to borrow ten pounds
● friends were trying to decide whether to go to the theatre or the pub for a night out
● they had to choose between travelling with convicts or waiting for the next coach.

Challenge pupils to think of similar scenarios.

Understanding character

Pip – ambitious choices **

Objective
● through shared discussion, to reflect on the growth and development of the protagonist in the course of a novel.

All of us make choices in our lives – we choose friends, we choose where we go, what we do and what we say. But we cannot choose our families and this was part of the problem for Pip, the central character in *Great Expectations*. The reader is not told what class he was born into, but at the opening of the novel, the seven-year-old Pip was an orphan being brought up by his only surviving sister and her husband, the village blacksmith. Pip was therefore working class and was expected to become an apprentice blacksmith when he was old enough. But Pip wanted more than this and through a series of events, he ended up becoming a gentleman. One of the conflicts for Pip was his view of his family. Through shared discussion of text extract 5.2 (*Pip – ambitious choices*) explore Pip's character using these questions:

Extract 1

- How was Pip expected to earn money?
- What was he going to do when he was older?
- He was writing a letter to Joe one evening. What does this tell the reader about his education?
- What is Dickens hinting at when Pip says he would like to be a scholar? How did Pip already feel about his future life?

Extract 2

- What do the word choices *common*, *coarse* and *thick* tell us about how Pip viewed Joe?
- Pip changed his view of life after visiting Miss Havisham and Estella. How does he now feel about becoming a blacksmith?
- Why did Pip want to be a gentleman?
- Pip looked down on Joe and his sister after visiting Miss Havisham. Whom did he blame for this? Did he ever think it was his own choice that might be the problem?

Extract 3

- What does the use of the one word *mean* tell the reader about Pip's view of his home?
- Why do you think he viewed being a gentleman as rising above his home and family?
- Did he seem upset about leaving home? Use evidence from the text to support your answer.
- What did he imagine he would do for Satis House and Estella?
- So, why did he say it was the loneliest night of his life?

Extract 4

- Explain the simile which Pip used to describe his hopes after he lost all his money.
- What words did he finally use to describe himself?
- In the end, what words show the reader that Pip understood the true value of Joe and his second wife, Biddy?

These questions are provided as discussion cards as resource 5.4 (*Ambitious choices*). Divide the class into four groups, giving one discussion card to each group. Then, bringing the class together, share outcomes of the group discussions.

Conclude by discussing the following questions:

- Was it wrong for Pip to be ambitious?
- How did he let money change him? Was it just about the money for Pip, or also about what other people would think of him?
- Whose choice was it to change?
- Is it wrong for people to be ambitious?
- How might the way other people see us be important to us?
- Can you think of examples of money changing people, for example, when they win millions on a lottery? How might their lives change? How might their families change? And how about their friends?

Although children's choices are limited, they will already have ideas about what they want to do when they grow up and the choices that they will need to make to achieve it. They will also have views about their families and how family members can play a part in their lives as they achieve their ambitions. To finish this activity, ask pupils to write about what they would like to do when they grow up. What are their Great Expectations for their own lives? Extend this by suggesting that pupils ask a parent to create a personal text, describing their Great Expectations for their child.

Abel Magwitch – hero or villain? * / **

> **Objective**
> ● to deduce the reasons for a character's behaviour through interrogation of the text.

Before deciding if the character of Abel Magwitch is a hero or a villain, pupils need to be able to understand his intentions. Chapter 42 contains a detailed description of Magwitch's early life. He is typical of the sort of criminal whose case Dickens argued for in much of his writing. Many Victorian children had to steal just to survive and it was not unusual for young children to be imprisoned or deported for such crimes. Dickens suggests that Magwitch was a victim of the social structure and therefore deserving as much of understanding as censure.

Read text extract 5.3 (*Abel Magwitch*) with pupils and explain that you are going to use the text to decide if Magwitch is a hero or a villain. To do this, use two drama activities, *Sculptor and sculpted*, immediately followed by *Thought tracking*. The aim is to understand why Magwitch acts in the way that he does – for example, would he really murder a child, or is he so hungry and desperate that he makes the threat to frighten Pip into co-operating? Use the activity cards in resource 5.5 (*Abel Magwitch*) for this, dividing the class into groups. Video each sculpture and thought track in sequence, then view the complete sequence of events as a class. Discuss what the drama activity has revealed about the intentions behind Magwitch's actions. Make a list of the different thoughts that he had.

Next provide each pupil with a piece of A3 paper. On one half, they should draw a portrait of Magwitch using paragraph one of the text extract. On the other half they should draw the outline of a head and write into it all of Magwitch's thoughts. Pupils can use the video and discussion as information sources for this; if the video is available on the school network, it can be referred to as often as necessary in order to capture all of Magwitch's thoughts.

Finally, as a class, try to decide if Magwitch was a hero, a villain, or possibly a little of both.

Dear Mum * / **

> **Objective**
> ● to infer the feelings of characters in a novel using evidence from the text.

Pip was an orphan, although Mrs Joe was his sister so he did live with a family member. Estella had no idea who her parents were and Miss Havisham adopted her as a baby at the suggestion of her lawyer, who was looking for a good home for an orphaned child. Neither Mrs Joe nor Miss Havisham was a kind or caring mother; even so, Pip and Estella's lives were much better than the alternative, which would have been the workhouse.

There are two text extracts available for this activity, one describing Miss Havisham (text extract 5.4) and the other describing Mrs Joe (text extract 5.5). You could use just one of the characters, use one as a model and the other for pupils to explore, or allow pupils to choose. Read one of the extracts, locating and discussing what sort of words Dickens chose to describe the character. Then provide pupils with a copy, asking them to mark in red all the words, phrases and statements that show the character to be unkind or uncaring, and mark in green all the positive aspects of the character. Which colour predominates? What does this tell the reader about the character?

Mrs Joe was attacked and permanently disabled by Orlick, a character who had worked at the forge prior to the attack. She took no further part in the narrative after the attack and died after Pip had moved to London and become a gentleman. Miss Havisham died in a terrible accident after Estella had grown up and married. Using the evidence in the text extracts, ask pupils to work in role as either Pip or Estella, writing a letter to Mrs Joe or Miss Havisham after their death, expressing their thoughts about their childhood. Sample letters for shared discussion or modelled writing are provided as resources 5.6 (*Letter to Miss Havisham*) and 5.7 (*Letter to Mrs Joe*).

Role on the wall * / ** / ***

Objective
- to use a drama strategy to explore characterisation.

Read Chapter 1. Then draw two large outlines of a male character, one labelled 'Pip' and one labelled 'The convict'. Pupils should interrogate the text to locate information about these two characters. Write comments on sticky notes and stick them on the appropriate outline. Information about appearance should be stuck around the outside of the outline. Information about internal characteristics such as personality or behaviour should be stuck inside the outline. So, for example, 'scared' would go inside Pip's outline while 'scruffy' would go outside the convict's. Encourage actual quotations using Dickens' text.

Using this information, discuss how Dickens creates such strong mental pictures of his characters. Perhaps emphasise this by substituting simpler words, examining phrases for effect. For example, would 'a scruffy convict' sound as effective as 'A fearful man, all in coarse grey, with a great iron on his leg'? Why, or why not? Add to the role on the wall as the narrative unfolds.

Puppet on a string **/ ***

Objective
- to understand how a character reacts under pressure.

This can be used at any point in the narrative when knowledge about a particular character has been built up. Think back over some of Pip's recent actions and decisions – make a list of them. Imagine that Pip is a puppet and you are his conscience; what would you say to him about the decision that he makes in each situation? Can pupils remember any situations when Pip's conscience has bothered him? On these occasions, has he listened to his conscience or allowed it to play any part in his decision making? What does this tell the reader about Pip?

Stages of expectation ***

> **Objective**
> - to analyse Pip's background and his development as a character.

Before reading each stage of *Great Expectations*, predict what you think will happen in each stage. Record ideas using resource 5.8 (*Stages of expectation*). When you have completed the reading of each stage, enter the actual events. Both predictions and recorded events should be supported with quotations from the text. Repeat this for each stage. How accurate were your predictions? In what ways did the narrative differ from your expectations? When all three stages are complete, review the entries and reflect on what you have learnt about Pip's development as a character in the course of the novel.

Love and rejection ***

> **Objective**
> - to explore the development of Pip as a character.

In any narrative, it is the dialogue which both moves action forward and also gives insight into characters and the reasons for their actions and behaviour. Divide pupils into groups, with each group studying either Chapters 11 and 12, or Chapters 13 and 14. Through close analysis, pupils should determine how Dickens uses language to describe Pip's thoughts and feelings and also how interaction is created with other characters. Then pupils should regroup so that each group contains people with information about all the chapters which have been read. Share information within each group, to compare and contrast Pip's thoughts and feelings about his life. Note key quotations.

> **Objective**
> - to consider Dickens' presentation of emotion through dialogue and the interaction of characters.

Read text extract 5.6 (*Love and rejection*), which is the conversation that Pip has with Estella and Miss Havisham when he visits them after Estella completes her education and returns home. Divide pupils into groups to perform a close analysis of the language of the dialogue. Each group should focus on either the interaction of Pip and Estella, or the interaction of Pip and Miss Havisham. Examine the author's vocabulary choices and the actions of the characters. How is the language different from the rest of the novel? What gives these conversations such intensity? What does it tell the reader about how Pip has changed in his behaviour? Have his feelings of inferiority changed? What new information does the reader learn about Miss Havisham's motivation and intentions towards both Pip and Estella?

When the close analysis is complete, regroup pupils so that each group has information about both Pip and Estella, and Pip and Miss Havisham. Share information within groups to build a complete picture of Pip's position in the relationship between Estella and Miss Havisham.

Understanding plot

Choices and consequences * / **

Objectives
- to use evidence from across a text to explain the decisions which a character makes
- to understand that actions have consequences.

Throughout the novel, Pip made a series of choices which created conflict and had consequences both for himself and other people. Text extract 5.7 (*Choices and consequences*) outlines two of the relationships through which Pip both creates conflict and learns about himself. Discuss this with the class. Give as an example the fact that Pip stole food to give to the convict. He was motivated by fear, as the convict had threatened to kill him if he did not help. Afterwards, he felt really guilty – he expected the police to turn up and arrest him at any time and he agonised over whether he should tell Joe what he had done. He was faced with a moral dilemma – steal or be killed. So did he make the right choice? This can be answered with a yes or a no, depending on your point of view. Ask pupils why he was right to steal (to protect himself and his family) and why he was wrong (because he should have told Joe that he had been threatened). Then discuss the consequences – for Pip this was a guilty conscience, for his family some missing food which was intended for the family's Christmas meal, and for the convict, the possibility of escape. There were even longer term consequences for Pip, as the convict then made it possible for him to become a gentleman.

Provide groups of pupils with a large sheet of paper for each group, on which they should create four columns. The first should be titled *Action*, the second *Good because*, the third *Bad because* and the fourth *Consequences*. Using resource 5.9 (*Choices and consequences*) ask pupils to cut up the boxes, discuss which box goes into which column and glue the boxes in place once a decision has been reached. If pupils are able to add further comments of their own, this would enrich the discussion. An answer sheet is also provided.

Conclude this activity by comparing the decisions each group has made. Discuss why choices are not always easy to make and how what we choose to do can have far-reaching consequences for other people, as well as ourselves. Can pupils think of instances when this has happened in their own lives?

Learning about myself * / **

Objective
- to understand the structure of a plot and the role of the protagonist in the narrative.

The plot of *Great Expectations* centres on Pip and what he learns about himself and those around him as he grows up. He makes some unkind decisions, gets into debt and becomes very proud. But through it, he learns to value people for who they are, not how they speak or how much money or status they have.

Resource 5.10 (*Learning about myself*) is a board game which reinforces the details of Pip's life. Working in pairs or small groups, pupils need a counter each and a die or spinner for the group. Take it in turns to throw or spin in order to move forward. When pupils land on a square, they earn or lose points depending on the action contained in that square. If the action is bad (coloured red) the person landing on it loses two points if it is something beyond their control and five points if it is the result of a bad decision that Pip made. Good squares are green, earning two points if the good action is someone else's and five points if the good choice is Pip's. Some squares are amber; these are neutral, as good and bad are balanced and so earn no points. The winner is the person with the least points at the end of the game.

Theatre and prison ***

> **Objective**
> - to examine Victorian social and cultural practices through the eyes of the novel's protagonist.

Text extract 5.8 (*Theatre and prison*) describes two visits which Pip makes. Ask pupils to read the extracts and list the questions which arise. Then, working in groups, pupils should discuss these questions, comparing the physical settings, the people involved and their emotions, reactions and behaviour. Some discussion questions are suggested below, to which pupils should add their own.

In the theatre:

- How does the audience's behaviour differ from a contemporary audience's at a production of Shakespeare?
- Did Victorians attend the theatre for different reasons from people who go to the theatre today?
- How do props and costumes differ?
- Why might Pip have wanted to avoid Mr Wopsle at the end of the performance?

In the prison:

- In what way does Mr Wemmick's sanguine attitude about the prisoners seem unusual?
- Why are prisoners offering him money?
- What is striking about his relationship with the prisoners?
- What do we learn about life in Victorian prisons?
- Why does Dickens describe Newgate prison as Mr Wemmick's greenhouse? What does this tell the reader?

To what extent might these descriptions be biased by Pip's personal viewpoint? Discuss how Pip might have reacted to the two situations. What do these extracts tell the reader about Victorian society?

Cost of living ***

> **Objective**
> - to investigate the social and historical context of the novel.

When Pip came of age, he was given an annual income of £500 a year. In the twenty-first century, that equates to about £35,000. Use resource 5.11 (*Cost of living*) to work out a monthly budget for living in 2012 London. Some choices have to be made about where to live based on rent and how to spend disposable cash. Then ask pupils to create a spreadsheet for a monthly budget in Victorian London. What different choices would need to be made about how to spend money? Two websites are suggested on the resource sheet which give some figures about Victorian costs of living.

Understanding setting

Family meals at Christmas * / **

> **Objective**
> ● to understand how a writer from a different time presents an experience.

This activity is also used in *A Christmas Carol* so could be linked in a cross-textual study of Dickens' descriptions of Victorian Christmas meals. A theme plan entitled *Celebrating Christmas* is available on the accompanying CD.

Christmas in the way that we celebrate it today was largely a Victorian invention. The Christmas family meal formed a central part of the celebration, although the food eaten would have been entirely dependent on the financial position of the family. Text extract 5.9 (*Christmas meals*) describes the Gargery family Christmas meal. Read through the extract with pupils and from it, list the food which the family ate – pickled pork, vegetables, roast fowl, mince pie, pudding and, finally, a savoury pie. What did they drink? Which items are similar to those we eat today and which are different? Is there anything unusual about the order in which the food was eaten? What does the presence of Uncle Pumblechook (there were also three other people with him) tell us about whom the Victorians liked to celebrate with? Can pupils track down all the examples of alliteration?

Ask pupils to draw a menu card for the Gargery Christmas meal. Then, if appropriate, draw a menu card for their own Christmas Day meal. What are the similarities? What are the differences?

Houses and homes * / **

> **Objectives**
> ● to explore Victorian houses and homes as described by one author
> ● to present information persuasively.

This activity is also repeated in the *Understanding setting* sections of *Bleak House*, *Hard Times* and *David Copperfield* so that the theme of houses and homes can be studied either in one book, or as a comparison of Victorian houses and homes across a range of texts. A theme plan, entitled *Houses and homes*, is available on the accompanying CD.

Text extract 5.10 (*Houses and homes*) contains Dickens' description of The Forge, where the Gargerys lived, and the unusual home of Mr Wemmick, a law clerk and friend to Pip. The website www.digitaldickens.com has a brief video of the forge at Chalk, in Kent, which is thought to be the inspiration for Joe Gargery's forge.

Through shared reading and discussion, find answers to the following questions.

- What sort of area was the forge built in? What would residents have been able to see from the windows of their home?
- What was the house built from? What were most houses of that time built from?
- What was the forge house like inside?
- What was unusual about Mr Wemmick's house? What DIY improvements had he made?
- Why do you think he added so much to his home?
- What was the garden used for?
- What would make this home attractive to other people?

Then ask pupils to use this information to write an estate agent's leaflet for each of the homes (resource 5.12 *For Sale*). Remember that the role of an agent is to show off the best points of the property in order to encourage people to visit it and, hopefully, purchase or rent it. Turn disadvantages into selling points – for example, Mr Wemmick's cottage and the door to get into it are very small, but Dickens still makes the home sound very attractive. How does he achieve this? How could that help when writing the estate agent's details?

Creating a setting – the moor * / **

> **Objective**
> - to explore how writers use language to create effect.

This activity is linked with *Bleak House* to create a cross-textual plan exploring weather as a setting. The theme plan, available on the accompanying CD, is called *Mr Dickens forecasts fog*.

Read text extract 5.11 (*The moor*) together. What sort of place does Pip live in? What can he see around him every day? For example, the extract describes the churchyard where his parents are buried, marshes, cattle, fields, the river and, in the distance, the sea. But there is an added dimension to this description, which is the effect of mist on an environment which Pip knows very well. The videos *Dickens' Kent* and *Saint James' Church* at www.digitaldickens.com have images of the moor and the churchyard.

After reading and discussing meaning, ask pupils, working in response pairs, to text mark as many examples as they can find of:

- powerful vocabulary
- noun and expanded noun phrases
- simile
- alliteration
- repetition
- personification.

List all suggestions and discuss how rich the language of this passage is. Then read the extract aloud – what makes the description so effective for the listener?

Through shared discussion, and using your school environment as a model, fill in the planning sheet resource 5.13 (*Creating a setting*). Include some of the things that you see every day, and then imagine that this familiar scene is turned into something different by a particular weather feature – mist, fog or a storm. The aim is to create the sort of suspense that Dickens creates in the extract which was analysed. Practise writing some similes – try to make them powerful enough to paint a picture in the readers' minds. In the planning boxes, list word choices which are examples of the language features analysed in the Dickens extract. Then model for your pupils how to write a similarly descriptive paragraph about your school. It should include familiar features which are made to appear quite frightening by a particular type of weather.

Brainstorm some vocabulary for different weather – for example, using a picture of fog, ask pupils to list as many words as they can which describe fog. Repeat this for other weather types. Then, using this shared vocabulary for support, ask pupils to write their own descriptive paragraphs. They will need to decide what environment they are going to use (home, school or an imaginary one) and how they are going to turn an everyday setting into one which is full of suspense. When the writing is complete, invite pupils to read their descriptions aloud. What is the effect of their writing on the listener?

Death and decay * / **

Objective

● to examine how language can be used to create visual effects in the mind of the reader.

Read text extract 5.12 (*Satis House*) aloud, one paragraph at a time. What are pupils imagining as they listen? Who might live in such a house? Why would they have allowed their house to decay to the point that it is crawling with insects? Why is there no daylight? Barred windows suggest a prison – what might this say about the person who owns the house? What sort of prison might they live in, with all the clocks stopped and all the light excluded? Why is there a crumbling wedding cake covered in cobwebs? Encourage pupils to both question and predict as you read the extract.

Next, divide pupils into groups, with about six people in each group. Explain that you are going to read the passage again, this time stopping at key points. When you stop, pupils must create a group sculpture portraying either an object or scene. So, for example, you might read '*Miss Havisham's house was of old brick, and dismal, and had a great many iron bars to it. Some of the windows had been walled up; of those that remained, all the lower were rustily barred. There was a courtyard in the front and that was barred*', before stopping and asking pupils to show a dismal house with barred windows. Allow three or four minutes for this, then share some sculptures. How effectively is the prison-like atmosphere portrayed? Next you might read, '*The garden was overgrown with tangled weeds. There was a clock in the outer wall that had stopped at twenty to nine*', and ask pupils to create this scene, including finding a way to portray the time on the stopped clock.

Continue through the extract, choosing key points at which children can create sculptures. Because of the time limit, problems have to be posed and solved very quickly. This encourages focus on the key words of the chosen sentences. Each time, invite one or two groups to share their work. Finally, discuss how this has deepened understanding of the setting. From this deepened understanding, try to define the sort of person who might live in this house and why that person might choose to live in this way.

As a writing response, invite pupils to create a setting without the character who belongs in it. How can words be used to create images in the reader's mind? Encourage pupils to read their setting descriptions to a response partner, asking the response partner what images and questions are raised in their minds as they listen.

Whole text responses

*Choral speaking * / ***

> **Objective**
> ● through collaborative working, use a drama strategy to explore the theme of a novel.

This activity uses a play structure from Greek tragedy, that of solo and chorus. The soloist in this case is Pip, with a small group forming the chorus, which fulfils the role of part conscience, part narrator. The class could be divided into groups so that there are several versions of this solo/chorus activity created. Rehearsal will be needed, as choral speaking is quite tricky to do well.

Below are ten statements from Pip's life. Provide these, and ask groups to write a choral response. So, for example, in response to Pip's first statement, 'I stole food to give to a convict. I felt so guilty that I expected to be caught and arrested,' the chorus might reply, 'You were very scared. You thought he would kill you. You were helping a starving man.' Discuss possible responses before starting group work – try to keep sentences short in the choral responses as this will make it easier to speak the lines in unison.

Pip's solo statements:

● I stole food to give to a convict. I felt so guilty that I expected to be caught and arrested.
● I was raised by hand – my sister was bad tempered and very unkind. It was her fault that I was sent to Miss Havisham and that I was always ashamed of my home after that.
● After I visited Miss Havisham and Estella for the first time, I really wanted to be a gentleman so that I could marry Estella. She laughed at me for having coarse hands and thick boots, but I have Great Expectations for my life.
● Joe was a good friend, but he was not educated and he did not have the manners of a real gentleman. I was terrified that Estella might see him and realise how common he was.
● After I was told that I was to become rich, I bought some fine clothes and showed them off to Joe and Biddy. I felt that they could have shown a little more respect to me.
● I took care to copy all that Herbert Pocket did so that I could stop being coarse. I was disappointed when Joe asked to visit – I was so ashamed of him that I would have paid him to stay away if I could.
● I got into debt because I spent so much money. I encouraged Herbert to spend a lot of money, too, even though he was not rich like I was. I did nothing about all the money that we owed.
● One day, the convict came back. He said that he was my benefactor and had worked hard in Australia so that I could be a gentleman. Why did he come here? He has destroyed all my hopes and put me in danger.
● With Herbert's help, we nearly saved Magwitch. But he was arrested. He was very weak and he died in prison. I had nothing. I was ruined and faced prison myself because of all my debt.
● Joe paid all my debts and saved my life when I was ill. I went to Egypt where I worked hard to pay Joe back. He was the finest person I ever knew and I treated him so badly.

This can be expanded if pupils have studied the book in enough depth to add further statements. Ask each group to stage dramatic readings of their play. Record them and create a podcast for other classes to listen to – this can be done at www.podbean.com.

Character blog ** / ***

> **Objectives**
> - to write in role to
>   - interpret the actions and behaviour of other characters through the eyes of the protagonist of a novel
>   - demonstrate understanding of characterisation, plot and an author's use of language to communicate
>   - demonstrate understanding of the social and cultural context of a novel from another time.

Throughout the study of *Great Expectations*, ask pupils to complete an extended writing task to run alongside the reading of the book. All significant events of the narrative will need to be blogged, supporting entries with as much of Dickens' language as possible. Set up a blog and include at least the following key events:

- Complete a detailed profile page for Pip.
- Focus on his thoughts and feelings after meeting Miss Havisham and Estella and how they highlighted and emphasised his position in society.
- Add his thoughts about the file and his nightmares.
- Reflect on his feelings after his sister is attacked.
- Explore his reaction to his conversation with Biddy about wanting to become a gentleman.
- Write an entry after his circumstances change. Use tone of address and language choices to show how superior he feels in contrast with his earlier entries.
- Reflect on his coach journey in the company of the convicts. What might he have thought and felt about this conversation?
- His reaction on receiving a large sum of money when he comes of age.
- Reactions to the discovery of his true benefactor.
- Reflect on his feelings when he realises that he has lost all his money and has nothing.
- Consider whether Pip believes that Miss Havisham is acting genuinely when she agrees to help Herbert Pocket.
- His feelings about his own kidnap.
- The changes he has gone through in the course of the novel and how he finally comes to value the true worth of his family.

Pip's views can be contrasted by including guest posts, for example from Magwitch, describing his thoughts when he is finally able to tell Pip what he has done for him. Include a guest blog from Estella, exploring her thoughts and feelings about her life and Miss Havisham's role in it.

Wiki discussion ***

> **Objective**
> - to consolidate knowledge of a complete text.

Pupils should create either a statement about one of the characters in the novel or a question involving one of the themes of the novel to use in a wiki discussion. This should then be added to the following five questions posted on a wiki discussion board to create a list of discussion topics.

- To what extent does Pip achieve his great expectations?
- How does Dickens use *Great Expectations* to make a statement on Victorian views about money and class?
- Is Pip the only character in the novel who has great expectations?
- Miss Havisham is misunderstood and should be pitied, not hated.
- Magwitch redeemed his earlier misdemeanours and should have been allowed to die a free man.

The back story ***

> **Objective**
> - to demonstrate knowledge and understanding of a novel.

Using all the information which has been gained about the character of Magwitch, write his back story. Review Chapters 1, 3, 5 and 42 in order to locate as much detail as possible. Chapter 42, in particular, details Magwitch's early life as he describes it to Pip. Alternatively, create the back story for Miss Havisham – information about her life can be found in Chapters 8, 11 and 22.

Pupils could also create a sequel for Pip and Estella. The ending of the story which is now published was not the original ending. In Dickens' first ending, Estella and Pip met again, but Pip no longer loved her, so they parted and there was no happy ending to their lives. He changed the original text after being persuaded that people would want to read a happy ending in which Pip eventually married a humbled Estella. A sequel would need to consider the changes that Estella would have to make to marry a man who is socially inferior and how Pip would also need to change in order to marry a woman whose social values he no longer believes in. What might the alternative ending have been? Pupils can use any medium to create a prequel or sequel.

⃝⃝⃝ Linked reading

Holes: Louis Sachar, Bloomsbury.
Mister Pip: Lloyd Jones, John Murray.
Al Capone Does My Shirts: Gennifer Choldenko, Bloomsbury.
Al Capone Shines my Shoes: Gennifer Choldenko, Bloomsbury.
Matilda: Roald Dahl, Puffin.
Boy and *Going Solo*: Roald Dahl, Puffin.
Knots in my Yo-Yo String: Jerry Spinelli, Alfred A. Knopf.
The Life and Times of the Thunderbolt Kid: Bill Bryson, Black Swan.

6 *Hard Times*

Overview

Context and social background

Dickens wrote *Hard Times* in 1854. In the hope that it would boost sales of the journal, it was published in weekly episodes in the paper, *Household Words*, which Dickens edited and published. The novel was published in book form in August 1854 when the serialisation was complete. Because it was written in weekly instalments, there are no subplots and descriptive detail is brief, so it is one of Dickens' shortest and most accessible novels.

Unlike many of his other books, which are set in London, *Hard Times* is set in Coketown, a fictitious town in the north, typical of the many factory towns which developed throughout the Industrial Revolution. Dickens' social comment centres around the uncaring morality of a middle class which aimed to make as much profit as possible as efficiently as possible. This is contrasted with the plight of the workers in mechanised factories. He also comments on a popular and growing utilitarian view which held that the ethical value of an action depended purely on how useful it was to the majority of people, or how much pleasure it gave.

A Victorian fascination with circus as a form of fantasy entertainment provides a useful vehicle to explore imagination in the novel. Hundreds of circuses operated in Victorian England, with trick horse riding, the skill of Mr Sleary in *Hard Times*, being one of the main attractions. Rare and exotic animals also featured. The type of tent with which we now associate circus performance was first introduced into Britain by a touring American circus troupe just ten years before *Hard Times* was written. Billed as the greatest show on earth, the American circus, Barnum and Bailey, immortalised in the musical *Barnum*, is probably one of the most famous of nineteenth-century circuses.

The workers in the Coketown mills of *Hard Times* formed a fledging trade union, although in the first half of the nineteenth century, when this novel was written, trade unions were still illegal – they were not finally legalised until 1871. The 1834 case of the Tolpuddle martyrs, in which six Dorset agricultural workers were sentenced to seven years' transportation for taking illegal oaths when forming a trade union, would have been in the minds of Dickens' readers. The national protests which swept England marked the start of the modern trade union movement.

There are also references in the novel to rail travel. Mr Bounderby buys a home at some distance from Coketown when it becomes accessible by train – the birth of modern commuting from the suburbs. The 1840s saw an explosion in railway construction as rural areas became increasingly urbanised. The railway became an important symbol of progress – a contemporary issue with which readers of *Household Words* would have been familiar.

Synopsis

The protagonist, Thomas Gradgrind, is a utilitarian industrialist living in the north of England. He runs a school, determined to prove that facts are all that are needed to be successful. Fancy (or wonder and imagination), represented by Mr Sleary's circus, is outlawed and the novel explores the tension created by 'fact' versus 'fancy'. Mr and Mrs Gradgrind have five children, the oldest of whom, Thomas and Louisa, play a central role in the narrative.

Tom and Louisa are educated in facts, with no room for imagination and wonder. When they show curiosity about a visiting circus, Mr Gradgrind is furious and employs Sissy, one of the circus girls, as a maid to his wife so that he can use the child in an educational experiment to prove that his philosophy works. As a result of their upbringing, Tom is very selfish and Louisa feels no emotion. When the banker Mr Bounderby proposes marriage, she agrees even though she does not love him, because she wants to further Tom's career in Mr Bounderby's bank.

One of the mill workers, Stephen Blackpool, is dismissed when he refuses to give Mr Bounderby information about the founding of a trade union at the mill. When a substantial sum of money is stolen from the bank, suspicion immediately falls on Stephen. Meanwhile, Louisa Bounderby has increasingly fallen under the spell of Mr Harthouse, a visitor to Coketown who wants to make Louisa fall in love with him for his own amusement. One night, while Mr Bounderby is away, he declares his love for Louisa, who immediately seeks refuge with her father.

Mr Gradgrind has realised that his education system is too rigid and when Mr Bounderby gives Louisa a few hours to return home, he takes pity on his daughter and she remains at Stone Lodge with him. When Stephen is found fatally wounded in an accident, Tom falls under suspicion of the theft. With the help of Sissy's circus friends, he escapes to live abroad, where he later dies of fever.

Main characters

- Thomas Gradgrind, a factory owner who also runs a school. He later becomes an MP
- Sissy (Cecilia) Jupe, daughter of a circus clown
- Thomas Gradgrind, son
- Louisa Gradgrind, daughter
- Josiah Bounderby, banker and friend of Mr Gradgrind
- Mr James Harthouse

Minor characters

- M'Choakumchild, the school master
- Mrs Gradgrind, wife
- Adam Smith, Malthus and Jane, the youngest Gradgrind children
- Mr Sleary, the circus owner
- Mr E.W.B. Childers, a circus performer
- Mrs Sparsit, Mr Bounderby's housekeeper
- Bitzer, a worker and messenger boy at the bank
- Rachael

Settings

- Stone Lodge, home of the Gradgrind family
- Coketown, a northern industrial mill town
- Sleary's Circus
- Mr Bounderby's bank
- Mr Bounderby's suburban home
- Stephen Blackpool's cottage

Themes

- Education
- Mechanisation and worker's rights
- Definitions of wealth and poverty
- Fact versus Fancy

Symbolism

- Stone
- Stairs
- Fire
- Pegasus

Activities

Hooks, starters and pause points

*I wonder * / ***

Sit pupils in a circle and start an 'I wonder' chain conversation. The first person says, 'I wonder what would happen if my mum won the lottery.' The next person has to suggest what might happen to them, then each person in turn adds a suggestion until ideas run out. At this point, the next person in the circle has to start another 'I wonder …' chain conversation.

Discuss how we are able to have these conversations – by using our imaginations. What else do we use our imaginations for? When reading, to bring a story to life, when watching a film, maybe imagining that we are part of the action, when playing games, when writing and when making up our own stories. Explain that the book *Hard Times* is partly about a family of children who were never allowed to wonder or imagine. Dickens uses the word 'fancy' instead of imagination. These children were only allowed to learn facts – nursery rhymes and storybooks were banned. Have children ever looked at a cloud and imagined it to be a monster or to have a face? The Gradgrind children, the family in the book, would not have been allowed to do this. Instead they would have had to learn facts about different cloud shapes and how and why clouds are formed. At one point in the story Louisa, the oldest girl in the family, is told off by her mother for staring into the flames of the fire and wondering about the future. The main character in the story, Mr Gradgrind, believed in facts so much that he started his own school where imagination was banned. How would today's pupils feel if they were never allowed to use their imaginations again?

*Graphic Hard Times * / ***

Watch the video clip at http://www.youtube.com/watch?v=j0Mqy8f2laA&feature=related. It introduces the major characters of the novel and some of its main themes. After watching the video, discuss what has been learnt about:

- the characters of Mr Gradgrind and Mr Bounderby
- what sort of school the children attend
- what Mr Gradgrind thinks about imagination and entertainment
- what sort of home the Gradgrinds live in.

Being for the Benefit of Mr Kite **

Pablo Fanque (real name William Darby) was one of the most successful nineteenth-century English circus owners. An advertising poster for his Circus Royal show can be found online at Wikipedia.org (http://en.wikipedia.org/wiki/File:Affiche_MrKite.jpg). One of the posters was bought by John Lennon in 1967 and he subsequently wrote the Beatles' song *Being for the Benefit of Mr Kite* (recorded for the *Sergeant Pepper's Lonely Hearts Club Band* album) based almost entirely on the poster.

Play pupils the track *Being for the Benefit of Mr Kite*. After listening for the first time, gather impressions about what the song might be describing. What has given them these ideas? Then listen to the track again, asking pupils to make a note of the names which they hear. At this point, show the poster and see how many of the names which they have noted can be found on the poster (the only difference is the name of the horse, which is Zanthus on the poster and Henry in the song). Mr Kite is believed to have worked for Pablo Fanque between 1843 and 1845. The Hendersons, John and his wife Agnes, were circus performers, specialising in trampoline acts, rope walking, clowning and trick horse riding. They performed across England and toured Russia in the 1840s and 1850s.

Listen to the song again. What creates the circus feel? Is it just the words? Or do the words and music support each other? Explain that Dickens' book *Hard Times* was written at the time when the Hendersons and Pablo Fanque's circus were at the height of their popularity and fame. Trick horse riding and clowning are two of the circus acts mentioned in *Hard Times*. Circus was a very popular form of entertainment and it plays a significant role in the narrative. Discuss why people like going to the circus, even today when there are many other forms of entertainment available. Why might it have been so popular for Victorian audiences?

Walking thesaurus ***

Give pupils a word which is related to a particular character, setting or aspect of the plot. Pupils must devise a thesaurus entry, finding as many alternatives to the given word as possible. For example, if you were studying the social background to *Hard Times*, you could provide the word 'revolution'. This activity encourages pupils to search their own vocabulary in order to find alternative definitions and also provides an opportunity to widen vocabulary through shared discussion.

Down-trodden operatives ***

Stephen Blackpool is included in the novel in order to articulate the debate surrounding working conditions and the rise of trade unionism in England. Resource 6.1 (*Down-trodden operatives*) provides an opportunity to consider the facts of the debate by reflecting on some incidents which led to the development of a legalised trade union movement in Victorian England. Discuss the information and in each case decide what the impact was on the social development of England.

- Why were trade unions necessary?
- Were the demands of the workers realistic and justified?
- What does the support of local communities say about the wider social view of pay and working conditions?
- How might increasing access to education and improved standards of literacy amongst the working classes have helped in spreading the union message?

Women's rights ***

Regardless of class, Victorian women had few of the rights that women in Britain enjoy today. Consider the following statements and discuss how they reflected the accepted social status of women:

- Single women and widows were allowed to own property and run businesses.
- Any property and any money which a woman owned became her husband's when she married.
- A married woman was not allowed to have a bank account.
- No women were allowed to vote in elections or be Members of Parliament.
- Women were allowed to go to university but were not allowed to graduate.
- In 1839, the law was changed so that women of good character whose husbands had divorced them were allowed access to their children.
- At the end of the Victorian era, 1.75 million women worked as servants and 200 were doctors.
- Many working-class women worked in factories and mills although girls in domestic service were only allowed to marry with the consent of their employer.
- Middle- and upper-class women were expected to marry and run their homes efficiently.

When reading *Hard Times*, pupils need to be aware of the social context in which the novel was written.

Understanding character

Vote for Gradgrind * / **

> **Objectives**
> - to deduce reasons for a character's behaviour from their actions and words
> - to show an imaginative response to a character's behaviour through writing in role.

Mr Gradgrind, the protagonist in the novel, has retired from the wholesale hardware trade in the fictional northern town of Coketown. He has built himself a house, he is married with five children and he also runs the local school, for which he has created a new model. Fancy, or imagination, is banned both in his school and his home. Facts are all that matter, so his children have not been allowed to learn nursery rhymes, they have only been taught facts. No storybooks have ever been allowed in his home. He hopes to persuade others of the value of factual education through the success of his model school.

His interest at the outset of the novel is to become an MP. In order to understand the character that Dickens has created in Mr Gradgrind, read and discuss the text extract 6.1 *Vote for Gradgrind*. What does Mr Gradgrind look like – is he literally square or is this a way of creating a particular picture in the mind of the reader? What is his philosophy? Why is he proud of his views? What does he hope to achieve by setting up a model school? Why does he get so cross about his children's fascination with the circus? Does fun ever play a part in Mr Gradgrind's life?

When the text has been discussed, ask pupils to highlight key words. There are then two tasks. The first is to prepare an election flyer about Mr Gradgrind – a sample text and blank template are provided as resources 6.2 (*Vote for Gradgrind exemplar*) and 6.3 (*Vote for Gradgrind template*). The flyer should contain a picture of the candidate (this would have been particularly important in Victorian times, when many people were unable to read) and his key beliefs. Evaluate the effectiveness of the posters against Dickens' own description.

The second activity is to work in role as Mr Gradgrind, preparing and delivering an election speech to explain his views in detail to an audience. Hot seating the character as groups or a class could help pupils rehearse the role before writing the speech. Although the genre for this is persuasive, plenty of exaggeration would be acceptable, as would negative comments about opposing views. For example, as well as explaining his own philosophy about facts, what might he say about other parents or teachers, who allow their children to learn nursery rhymes and draw pictures? What would he think about a school which allowed its teachers to share poetry with the pupils? And what might he have to say about people who have flowers on their carpets or birds and butterflies on their china? A model text is provided as resource 6.4 (*Mr Gradgrind's speech*). Pupils could then stage a meeting in which they present their speeches to a class which has not been involved in this activity. Would the audience vote for Gradgrind? If so, why? If not, why not?

Find him on Facebook * / **

> **Objectives**
> ● to deduce reasons for a character's behaviour from his actions and words
> ● to show an imaginative response to a character's behaviour through writing in role.

Josiah Bounderby, the Coketown banker, regarded himself as a self-made man. He was Mr Gradgrind's closest friend and never wasted an opportunity to impress the Gradgrind family, and anyone else who cared to listen, about his rags-to-riches life story. He often painted a picture of himself as a neglected, deserted child, raised by a drunken grandmother until he ran away, working his way from 'vagabond, errand boy, labourer, porter, clerk, chief manager and small partner', to Josiah Bounderby of Coketown. He claimed to have taught himself to tell the time from the clock on the steeple of St Giles Church in London and to read from the letters on shop signs. Is he justly proud of his achievements, or is there another reason for his constant boasting? Find out about Mr Bounderby in Dickens' words in the first section of text extract 6.2 (*Find him on Facebook*). A reading of this section is also available on http://www.youtube.com/watch?v=DSSK-m3-xGU&feature=related.

Before starting individual work, use improvisation games to get behind the character's thinking. Mr Bounderby never wastes an opportunity to boast about his deprived start in life and how he worked his own way up to wealth and social position. Working in pairs or groups, improvise some conversations he might have – every conversation has to refer to his past in some way, to make himself seem important despite his inferior start in life. Below are some suggested situations in which Mr Bounderby found himself in the novel which could form the basis of the improvisations:

● his housekeeper talks with him about visiting an Italian opera as a child
● he visits Mr Gradgrind to ask if he can marry Louisa
● he offers a job to Tom Gradgrind
● he meets Stephen Blackpool to discuss the new union which is being formed at the mill.

Then, prepare a Facebook profile for Mr Bounderby, using evidence from the first section of text extract 6.2. What tone would his profile use? What would he most want readers to know about himself? Why would he not provide any information about his favourite music? If film had been invented, why would he not have had any favourite films? What sort of books would he include as his favourite titles?

Finally, read the section in text extract 6.2 which describes Mr Bounderby's mother. If she chose to comment on his Facebook profile, what would she say?

Conscience alley **

> **Objectives**
> ● to understand reasons for conflict
> ● to use a drama strategy to explore the moral dilemma of a character.

Stephen Blackpool represents one of the moral dilemmas of the mid-nineteenth century. In response to workplace deaths and accidents, child labour and the poor housing conditions of factory and mill workers, unions were beginning to form to represent the rights of workers. Unions were still illegal when *Hard Times* was written and membership could lead to transportation. Today we take issues of safety at work and employee welfare seriously, but in Victorian times many mill and factory owners were much more interested in productivity than safety. The debate is played out in this novel. The mill owner, Josiah Bounderby, firmly believed that workers just wanted to eat '*turtle soup and venison with a gold spoon*', and this informed his decisions in running the mill and housing the workers. Far from exploiting his workers, he felt that they were trying to exploit him. He cared nothing for the fact that by sacking Stephen Blackpool, he would be condemning him to homelessness and probable starvation.

Stephen Blackpool refused to join the union, although he said that this was for personal reasons. He saw the union representative as just using the workers' suffering to create conflict with Mr Bounderby, which could only lead to harm for the members. As a result of his refusal to join, the other workers in the mill sent him to Coventry, refusing to have anything to do with him – a view of social solidarity which still continues today. What Stephen was asking for was the right to make up his own mind and follow his conscience.

Read text extract 6.3 (*Conscience alley*). There are two issues of conscience to be explored. The first is Stephen's refusal to join the union even though he knows what the cost will be. The second is Mr Bounderby's attempt to get Stephen to spy for him, when he discovered that Stephen had been isolated by his fellow workers. Divide the class into two groups, giving one of the dilemmas to each group. One group should interrogate the text to find reasons why Stephen should, and should not, join the union, then explore these in *Conscience alley*. To do this, divide the group into two lines, with one person acting in role as Stephen Blackpool. As the character walks between the two lines, one side of the alley should give reasons why Stephen should join the union and the other side should give reasons why he should not join. The other group should find reasons why Stephen should, and should not, inform on his colleagues to the mill owner, and do the same. After rehearsal, perform both *Conscience alleys*. What did Stephen decide to do and why? Is the outcome supported by the text?

As a writing outcome, ask pupils to write in role as Stephen, blogging about his experience. It should reflect both sides of the dilemma and the reasons for his choice. A sample text is provided as resource 6.5 (*Stephen Blackpool's blog*), but this would be a powerful task if a class blog was used, so that feedback comments could be made immediately both within the class and a wider community audience.

LinkedIn ***

> **Objective**
> ● to explore Dickens' characterisation through his use of language.

Using text extract 6.4 (*LinkedIn*), ask pupils to highlight all the words which Dickens has used to describe Mr Gragrind. What impression do these words create in the mind of a reader? Why did Dickens make these word choices? What did he want to communicate? Write a paragraph explaining your views on the effective use of language to create character. Support your thoughts with quotations and evidence from the text. Then, create a LinkedIn profile for Gradgrind using all the information which you have acquired about him. Emphasise what he most wants to be known for – the importance of Facts over Fancy, or imagination.

The Bully of humility ***

> **Objective**
> ● to understand how a character can be created to comment on a social context.

Use text extract 6.5 (*The Bully of humility*) to analyse the character of Mr Bounderby. Use this information to create a character profile. Choose one word to summarise his personality. His view of Louisa is mentioned twice. Why might this be important? What might it be foreshadowing?

Finally, discuss how the character of Bounderby is a comment on Victorian society – reference to *Life in Victorian England (Understanding plot)* would facilitate this. Include Gradgrind in the discussion. Both of these characters have been created by Dickens to serve a particular purpose in the book. What message is Dickens giving to the reader? How might this be pursued further in the novel? End by creating a predictions sheet for the book.

The role of women ***

> **Objective**
> ● to understand the role of women in the narrative of *Hard Times*.

Working in pairs, choose one of Louisa Gradgrind, Sissy Jupe or Mrs Sparsit.

Decide why Dickens included these women in the story – what role does the chosen character fulfil? Consider the work which they do and the expectations of the men around them. What relationship do they have to the plot? Refer to the text for evidence to support views.

Then regroup into threes, so that each group of three has a representative for each of the three women. Use a triple role on the wall to compare the lives, characters and roles of these women. Underneath each name, write one sentence which summarises their role in the novel so far. Share ideas and then create a class sentence for each woman. Retain sentences for review as the novel progresses.

Mrs Sparsit's staircase ***

> **Objective**
> ● to consider Dickens' use of the novel to make moral statements about a character.

Read *Reaping* Chapter 10 (26)[1] and draw an image of a staircase which both rises and falls. What does Mrs Sparsit think about Louisa? What motivates her to spy on Louisa and delight in seeing her descent towards ruin? Plot Louisa's social rise and impending fall. In another colour, plot her impending moral fall. Then write underneath the image a prediction about what will happen to her a) socially and b) morally by the end of the novel.

Use a *Conscience alley* for Louisa, persuading her either that she should stay with Bounderby or leave him. If the outcome is to leave, create a second alley to decide whether Louisa should leave him to return home to her father or leave him to elope with Harthouse. Remember the morals and opinions of the time in which Louisa lived. Would the same conclusion be reached if contemporary social values were applied?

MP's apology ***

> **Objective**
> ● to examine how Dickens uses language to show changes in character.

Read *Garnering* Chapter 1 (29). Compare the language which Mr Gradgrind uses in this chapter with his language in *Sowing* Chapter 1. What is different about his use of English? Why has Dickens done this? Write a paragraph explaining how Dickens has used language to show the changes in a character.

Create a press release for Gradgrind to give to local journalists explaining his change in views and reasons for the change. Knowledge from *Create a campaign (Understanding plot)* would be beneficial. Ask pupils to present their press releases and talk in role to take questions about the philosophy that they are outlining. Encourage the use of quotations and use evidence from the text to answer questions.

Louisa: person or property? ***

> **Objective**
> ● to examine Dickens' view of the attitudes of men towards women in Victorian society.

Familiarise pupils with *Garnering* Chapters 2 and 3 (30 and 31) and discuss the following:

● How is Mr Harthouse presented during Sissy's visit?
● Does he really care about Louisa or is she just a distraction for his amusement?
● How does he react to Louisa's decision not to see him again?
● Does he show respect for Louisa at any time in the novel?
● What leads the reader to this conclusion?
● Is there any evidence that Mr Bounderby cares about Louisa as a person?

- How does the reader form an opinion of Mr Bounderby's view of marriage?
- Does he demonstrate any respect for Louisa's need for peace and some time alone?
- What do his final actions say about his view of his wife?

Create a presentation to show how Harthouse and Bounderby treat Louisa and their reactions to her decisions. Presentations must include at least three quotations, at least one of which is a contrasting quotation taken from earlier in the novel. Share presentations with the class and be prepared to explain why particular quotations were chosen and what evidence there is in the text to support this viewpoint.

In Memoriam Stephen Blackpool ***

Objective
- to understand the purpose of a particular character in a novel.

Think about how our society marks the death of a person. How is the life of the dead person celebrated? What do we want to remember about them? Are everyone's memories the same or does it depend on relationship? Consider all that is known about Stephen Blackpool – his character, the way he interacted with other workers, his refusal to spy on other people at the mill, his drunken wife and his love for Rachael. Create a short movie entitled '*In Memoriam* Stephen Blackpool' to celebrate his life and the person that he was. Use images, music, poetry and any comments that his friends might have made about him.

Conclude by discussing why the character was included in the novel. What did Dickens want the character to represent? How successful is this?

How the mighty have fallen ***

Objective
- to explore how Dickens uses a character to make social and moral points.

Mr Gradgrind undergoes a significant change in his views in the course of the novel. Plot his rise and fall using resource 6.6 (*How the mighty have fallen*). Different colours could be used to represent his social views and the moral issues which affect him. Once completed, this will provide an overview of the character of Mr Gradgrind and demonstrate visually how Dickens uses the character to make social and moral points.

Understanding plot

Mantle of the expert – should children work? **

Objectives

● to explore a complex issue through working in role
● to work logically and methodically to test ideas and make deductions
● to write discursively, using points which emerge through debate.

Mantle of the expert is a drama strategy developed by Dorothy Heathcote to encourage an enquiry-based approach to learning. Pupils are placed in a situation in which they must work in an expert role to investigate or research a particular aspect of the situation. In this activity, pupils will work as commissioners and well-known Victorian figures in order to investigate child labour, with particular reference to mills, factories and the coal mines that produced coal to fuel the machinery. In 1841, the government set up a commission to examine the issue of child labour in which workers and employers were interviewed: pupils will be invited to become commissioners in order to conduct the interviews and visits. Six eminent Victorian people will also be interviewed. They will then prepare and deliver speeches in role to the Commission, which will hold a debate before reporting to Parliament in preparation for possible changes to legislation.

Explain the issue of child labour – during the Industrial Revolution, thousands of families left the countryside, where they had worked as farm labourers, to find work in the new factories and mills. Children started work as young as five or six years of age. Education was neither free nor compulsory, so children from poor homes worked in order to contribute to the family income – wages were so low for manual work that everyone in the family worked if possible. In addition, life expectancy was short, so children were frequently left orphaned to either enter the workhouse or fend for themselves. Housing was often inadequate and overcrowded as so many people had to be housed in towns and cities in order to keep industry working. Employers – the factory, mill and mine owners – ranged from those who provided some education for their workers' children and built adequate housing, to those whose only motivation was the development of their businesses. Mr Bounderby, in *Hard Times*, is an example of the latter, with his view that workers just wanted to eat turtle soup and venison using gold spoons. Since there was no legislation to protect the health and safety of children, conditions were entirely dependent on employers' personal decisions. Although conditions gradually improved, it took thirty years from the first Commission for a child's working day to be limited to ten hours and a further ten years before primary education became free and compulsory for all children up to the age of ten.

Dickens was a great supporter of the view that children should be educated and that the working and living conditions of the poor should be improved. This was born out of personal experience, as Dickens was forced to leave school and go out to work himself when just a child, when his father was imprisoned in Marshalsea Debtors Prison for non-payment of debt. Pupils will research the working conditions of children who worked in the mills, factories and mines, and then study the views of six people who engaged in the developing debate. Then, working in role as one of the six people, they will prepare a contribution to a public debate explaining their view of child labour and why they hold that view.

Start by reading the *Letter to the Commissioners* in resource 6.7 – this would have more impact if it was delivered as an email to the class. Discuss the task and provide the research materials for the Commissioners to make their visits and collect evidence (resource 6.8,

Resources for Commissioner visits to mills). Through shared discussion, remaining in role, establish what information has been collected during the visits.

In the second part of the activity, allocate one Victorian person to each group, asking pupils to research this person and find out what they thought about child labour (resource 6.9 *Research cards for child labour debate*). One person in each group will change their role from Commissioner to the given character. Commissioners should interview the character, forming questions from their research. They should then use this information to prepare a speech which will be delivered to the full board of Commissioners in order for the Commission to report to Parliament. The law may, or may not, be changed to protect children, depending on their speeches.

Then, the six Victorian people should deliver their speeches with the rest of the class remaining in role as Commissioners. A debate can then be conducted to decide how the Commission should report to Parliament. Remember that they must work in role and in context – they cannot suddenly suggest that all children should go to school instead of going to work, as there would not have been enough schools or teachers for this to happen. In addition, British industry would have collapsed without child workers, so any changes would have been made slowly. What is the first priority of the Commission? How will they suggest that this is dealt with by Parliament?

Finally, working independently in role as a Commissioner, pupils should bring together all of this information to write a discursive report outlining both sides of the argument. Recommendations for changes can also be made – a sample text is provided as resource 6.10 (*Report of the Commission Investigating Child Labour*).

Transport * / **

> **Objective**
> ● to explore how a writer from a different time uses language and presents experiences.

This theme is also explored in the *Understanding setting* section of *David Copperfield*, so this can be studied within one book, or across both texts to gain a wider picture of Victorian transport. A theme plan entitled *Transport* is available on the accompanying CD.

By the time *Hard Times* was written, most major towns in England could be reached by rail. This had a significant impact on mobility, as people could travel further afield. The railway was also controversial because of the amount of land which was consumed in the building of it. Pupils can investigate the effect of the railway on trade and commerce by playing a game at http://www.show.me.uk/hosted/networks/networks.swf in which they will have to select the most efficient mode of transport to move goods around ready to be traded.

The railway forms an integral part of the plot in the novel. Josiah Bounderby chooses to purchase a house some distance from Coketown, enjoying the clean air of the country and commuting to the mill and the bank by train. Louisa also uses the train to escape the attentions of James Harthouse and return to her father's home at Stone Lodge. As an MP, Mr Gradgrind would have commuted between London and Coketown with more ease than coach travel afforded. The train and the mill machinery also represent the mechanical developments of the Industrial Revolution.

Read the extracts from *Hard Times* which mention the railways (resource 6.11 *Transport*). There are some discussion questions to share. Then investigate what sort of words Dickens used to describe the railway – *iron, fire, steam, smoke* and the onomatopoeic *hiss, shriek* and *crash*. Verb choices include *trembling*, *tearing*, *glaring*, *shrieking* and *rattling*. What do these word choices suggest about Dickens' view of the railway?

In response to these words, pupils can either:

● design an onomatopoeia poster using one of the sound words in the text, illustrating the sound of the word by shape and colour

or:

● list the interesting and powerful words which Dickens uses about the train and make a word cloud at www.wordle.com. This creates a clear graphic representation of the words. Colour and font can be manipulated to match the required image.

Life in Victorian England ***

> **Objective**
> ● to understand the social background to a novel from another time.

Working in groups, ask pupils to research one of the following topics:

● utilitarianism
● Victorian child labour laws
● work life in the Industrial Revolution
● travel during the Industrial Revolution
● daily life during the Industrial Revolution
● the emergence of the middle class
● the Great Exhibition and curiosity about new ideas
● Victorian education.

Pupils should produce an informative PowerPoint presentation containing two or three slides to present to the rest of the class. When viewing the presentations, remind pupils to take notes in order to build a clear picture of the changes which were happening in society.

What's in a name? ***

> **Objective**
> ● to consider how narrative structure and plot relate.

Look at the contents listing for *Hard Times* – it is a tri-partite novel. Through shared discussion, answer the following questions:

● What did Dickens name the three parts of *Hard Times*?
● A verse from the Bible (Galatians Chapter 6 verse 7) says 'For whatsoever a man soweth, that shall he also reap'. How did this inspire the structure of the book?
● What might the implications of this structure say about Dickens' intentions for his novel?
● Didactic literature is intended to teach the reader about a particular moral or religious theme. What might the theme of this novel be?
● How do the words chosen as the title of each book communicate Dickens' possible theme?

Following the discussion, invite pupils to write a paragraph explaining how the structure of the book demonstrates Dickens' intentions to his reader.

Next, discuss the potential titles that Dickens considered for this novel, before settling on *Hard Times*. He sent all 14 suggestions to a friend to ask him which ones he preferred – Dickens himself had three favourites: *Hard Times*, *A Mere Question of Figures* and *The Gradgrind Philosophy*.

Working in pairs, suggest three ideas for what the book might be about, based on the suggested titles.

- *According to Cocker*
- *Prove It*
- *Stubborn Things*
- *Mr Gradgrind's Facts*
- *The Grindstone*
- *Hard Times*
- *Two and Two are Four*
- *Something Tangible*
- *Our Hard-headed Friend*
- *Rust and Dust*
- *Simple Arithmetic*
- *A Matter of Calculation*
- *A Mere Question of Figures*
- *The Gradgrind Philosophy*

Finally, create a predictions sheet for the novel, using these suggested titles to inform the possible content of the novel.

Create a campaign ** / ***

> **Objective**
> - to explore the social context in which *Hard Times* is set.

Creating a media campaign can explore the social context of *Hard Times* through the eyes of one of the central characters. Mr Gradgrind has a clear philosophy of life which he is attempting to work out through his parenting and the way he runs his school. Bounderby typifies the new middle-class, self-made man that the Industrial Revolution created.

Choosing one of these characters, create a media campaign which should include a 60-second advertisement explaining their philosophy of life. Posters and flyers should also be created to distribute at political rallies and meetings. Resource 6.12 (*Create a campaign*) will support pupils.

Present and evaluate the campaign materials for each group.

- How accurately have the character's views been represented?
- How has language been used to communicate?
- How persuasive are the materials?
- What would the modern equivalents of these campaigns be?
- Are any of these topics relevant to the twenty-first century?

Little pitchers ***

> **Objective**
> ● to examine Dickens' portrayal of childhood in the novel.

The three children in the novel, Tom, Louisa and Sissy, are described by Dickens as 'little pitchers' waiting to be filled with information and facts. The children often intimate that they have a different view of themselves and what they would like their childhood to be. The chart in resource 6.13 (*Little pitchers*) examines the different points of view of the children. An example in the first row of the chart shows how a statement is discussed and evidence is noted. Pupils can add their own statements if they wish. When the chart is complete, discuss what picture this gives the reader of the children's view of themselves as little pitchers waiting to be filled.

Stephen's women ***

> **Objective**
> ● to consider the social and historical background to the novel.

Chapters 10 and 11 detail Stephen's relationships with his estranged wife and Rachael, a lady with whom he works. He would like to divorce his wife and marry Rachael, so he decides to ask for advice from Mr Bounderby, his employer. Unfortunately he is told that divorce is a luxury for the rich and there is nothing he can do. Analyse Stephen's relationships with the two women using resource 6.14 (*Stephen's women*) to show the advantages and disadvantages of both relationships. What does this section of the novel tell the reader about Victorian views about marriage and divorce, particularly as it related to the working classes?

The Jeremy Kyle show ***

> **Objective**
> ● to explore the issue of working-class life in a novel from another time.

Working in groups, create and title a sketch for the Jeremy Kyle show. The sketch should include Stephen Blackpool, Mr Bounderby, Rachael and Stephen's wife. Use the information from Chapters 10 and 11 of *Sowing*. Discuss the angle that each group has chosen. When complete, watch and film each sketch. Discuss the content – how truthful is the content to the book? How effectively have the issues surrounding working-class people in Victorian life been portrayed? What do the sketches say about class difference and equality? Have any new questions been raised about social context?

Cause and effect ***

> **Objective**
> ● to examine the effectiveness of the structure of the novel.

Resource 6.15 (*Cause and effect*) is a table which can be used at any point when a review of the plot is needed. The first line is completed as an example. A cause and effect chart can be used as a single or ongoing activity throughout the study of the novel. Resource 6.16 (*Crossed lines*) also provides a resource for plotting the novel, using a line for each character and setting to show interaction.

This house believes ***

> **Objectives**
> ● to examine Dickens' use of language to demonstrate social issues
> ● to use the language of debate when writing and speaking in role.

Using text extract 6.6 (*This house believes*) examine the speech which the visiting trade union-ist makes at the beginning of *Reaping* Chapter 4 (20). Analyse Dickens' use of language to establish why this speech is so powerful. In an age when few working-class people could read, rhetoric was a vital means of persuasion and propaganda. Compare this with Bounderby's conversation with Stephen Blackpool where he is trying to persuade him to provide information about the workers. What kind of language does Dickens use here? How is it different? Is it more or less effective? Why? What does Bounderby use to persuade rather than language and reason? What clues are there to this in the text?

In response, write in role as Stephen Blackpool. Write a journal entry for each of the encounters he has – hearing the initial speech, refusing to join the union along with the subsequent reactions, making his own speech and his encounter with Mr Bounderby that ends in his dismissal. Then, prepare a speech and hold a class debate. The motion is 'This house believes that union membership is a matter of personal conscience'. Was Stephen Blackpool right to act as he did? Thinking back to the language studied in the text extract, what devices could be used in a speech to make it more persuasive? Today, pay and working conditions are agreed for all employees regardless of union membership. In Victorian times, when working conditions were so poor and wages were low, power of numbers was important for the success of fledging unions. Try to consider the social context in which Dickens was writing – when *Hard Times* was written, union membership was still criminalised.

Conclude by holding a ping-pong debate – on one side of the classroom stand all the people who agreed that Stephen was right to act as he did and on the other side, all those who agreed with the workers and/or Bounderby. The first pupil makes a point and someone on the opposite side steps up and rebuts the comment with an opposing statement. At the conclusion of the activity, have a show of hands to determine the majority view.

The gossips go to town ***

> **Objective**
> ● to explore how Dickens use the structure of a novel to make a moral statement to the reader.

Read *Garnering* Chapter 5 (33) from '*Some train had newly arrived in Coketown*' to the end of the chapter. Then pupils should work in role, imagining that they are a mill worker or a servant gathering at the pub as the news spreads through town that the mysterious old woman who has been seen waiting outside Bounderby's house is actually his mother. His whole life is revealed as a lie. Create a drama to show how different people would react to the news. How might Rachael feel, since Bounderby was responsible for the circumstances that led to Stephen's death? Would they have spoken about Bounderby differently behind closed doors? How pleased would the mill workers be that he has been found out? Perform and discuss the dramas. Does everyone have the same reaction to the news? Why might some people think differently from others? What emotions are expressed?

Discuss why Bounderby created the lies about his childhood. What was he hoping to achieve? Why did Dickens create this plot line? What moral point was he making to the reader?

Understanding setting

School days * / **

> **Objectives**
> ● through shared discussion, to interrogate a text describing a school setting
> ● to compare this setting with the reader's current experience
> ● to write a chronological recount, using knowledge and information from group and class discussions, and research.

This activity is also repeated in the *Understanding setting* section of *David Copperfield*, so that the theme can be studied either in one book, or as a comparison of Victorian schools across a range of texts. A theme plan entitled *School days* is available on the accompanying CD.

Mr Gradgrind started the school in Coketown to prove his principle of Fact versus Fancy. His own five children had never been allowed to exercise their imaginations and had been instructed in facts from a young age. His view was progressive in more than one way, as his daughter, Louisa, was educated on an equal footing with her brothers.

In his school, facts were all that mattered. Children had numbers rather than names and he saw their minds as empty pots which just needed filling with facts. He employed M'Choakumchild as the school teacher. It contrasts strongly with those schools described in *David Copperfield* and *Great Expectations*. A range of children were clearly admitted, as Sissy Jupe, a circus child, was present in the school and was called on to present facts. There is no suggestion that the children were punished and there was a genuine concern about shaping their knowledge. In fact, Mr Gradgrind was so sure of the value of his experimental education that when Sissy's father disappeared, he employed her as a maid so that he could educate her according to his principles. The experiment, of course, failed, and Mr Gradgrind found through the breakdown of his daughter's marriage that a diet of nothing but facts does not equip a child for the emotional demands of life – what would today be described as emotional literacy.

Read the brief text extract 6.7 *School days*. Then look at http://www.bl.uk/learning/images/dickens/large116573.html, which contains an example of the type of book that would have been used in a school such as Gradgrind's. It is a Railway ABC, which would have served two purposes, one as a primer to teach the alphabet and the other to teach facts about the new railways that were built across the country.

Click on Victorian schools/Victorian children in the Activities section/School and Learning at the website http://www.bbc.co.uk/schools/primaryhistory/victorian_britain/ to find an example of a Victorian school log book, which all schools kept. There is also a video of the school diary. Read the log book entries – how do they differ from schools today? How did Mr Gradgrind's school differ from your own? After studying the evidence ask pupils to write two log book entries, one in role as M'Choakumchild and one about their own school. Contrast the two schools. It would be interesting if you as the teacher also wrote in role as M'Choakumchild and as yourself. Compare the outcomes with those of your pupils.

Those dark satanic mills **

> **Objectives**
> - to understand how a writer from a different time presents experience
> - to reflect differences between past and present experience by creating a contrast poem.

This phrase is taken from William Blake's poem 'And did those feet', which has been popularised as the hymn *Jerusalem*. It refers to the mills which were built during the Industrial Revolution and the poem was felt to reflect the atmosphere of the mills and the lives of those who worked in them.

Show pupils an image of a typical red brick mill such as the Ancoats mill complex in Manchester. An image of the type of mill that Dickens would have seen when visiting Manchester can be found at http://www.englishheritageimages.com. Although images can give an impression of the size of the buildings, most Victorian mills have been adapted for other use and so are now surrounded by blue skies and clear canal water. In order to understand how polluted the air was by the smoke, steam and ash pouring from the many chimneys, pupils will need to visualise Dickens' description.

Read the text extract 6.8 *Those dark satanic mills* and mark any words that create a picture in the mind of the reader, or words which are particularly powerful. Then choose five or six of the powerful images in Dickens' description. Resource 6.17 (*Those dark satanic mills contrast poem*) demonstrates how to use these phrases or words on a planning grid. Next, brainstorm some other powerful words which are suggested by the visualisation – some examples are written in italics on the planning grid. Review knowledge and understanding of figurative language, particularly simile and metaphor. Finally, working either in pairs or individually, write some poetic sentences using the words and phrases from the planning grid. Read poems aloud, encouraging pupils to listen carefully and make suggestions for development.

Ask pupils to repeat this with images from their own surroundings. This will create a second verse for the poem. How well do the two verses of the poem portray Dickens' setting of the mills, which Blake described as dark and satanic, and the children's own modern environment? What can we learn about Victorian city life? How have our environments changed?

This sample text (also provided as resource 6.17) could be read to great effect by two readers alternating the lines from each verse – this makes the contrast even stronger.

A fog of drifting ash hides jagged lines of crimson brick.
The silent, still canal lies black in careless death
And poisoned purple water slowly chokes on evil smelling dye.
The serpent coils of thick black smoke wind endlessly around the sky,
As chimney stacks reach high to hide the shrouded sun.
And footsteps drag through heavy ash and leave a grimy trail of mist and rain.

Green and lofty trees wave softly in the gentle breeze,
Streams of clear, pure water bounce and bubble over stony river beds,
Fish dart and leap like silver swords through sparkling water
Fresh, clean air breathes purity and life into each day.
Dappled sunlight warms the earth in gentle beams
And footsteps trail through snowy paths or kick a path through fallen leaves.

Houses and homes * / **

Objectives

- to explore Victorian houses and homes as described by one author
- to compare and contrast Victorian and contemporary houses and homes.

This activity is also repeated in the *Understanding setting* sections of *Bleak House*, *Great Expectations* and *David Copperfield*, so that the theme can be studied either in one book, or as a comparison of Victorian houses and homes across a range of texts. A theme plan, entitled *Houses and homes*, is available on the accompanying CD.

Two homes are described in text extract 6.9 (*Houses and homes*), Mr Gradgrind's impressive home which he designed and built and the one-room home of the mill worker, Stephen Blackpool. Read the text extracts and discuss the differences.

- What do the homes of each man say about their relative wealth and social position?
- How might an estate agent find a positive angle when attempting to find a tenant for Stephen Blackpool's room after he left Coketown?
- Why were streets of similar housing built by mill owners?
- How important was it that workers lived very near to the mill?
- Why did Mr Gradgrind choose to live on a moor two or three miles from the town?
- What did he want to get away from?
- How could this be used as a unique selling point by an estate agent?
- Why did the distance from town not matter?
- Why did Mr Gradgrind have a beautiful garden when Stephen had none?

Design estate agents' leaflets for each of these homes, finding the positive angle even on the single-room home. Then compare the two homes – what do they tell us about wealth and poverty in Victorian times? Resource 6.18 *For sale* provides a template.

The circus comes to Coketown ***

> **Objectives**
> - to compare and contrast two settings
> - to consider why the author has created these contrasts.

Using text extract 6.10 (*The circus comes to Coketown*) compare the two key settings of the novel – the circus and Coketown. Circus was a popular form of entertainment in Victorian times and travelling circuses were common. Analyse the text and consider the language which Dickens has used in creating one of these settings. Locate key quotations, then pair with a person who has analysed a different setting. Through shared discussion, decide how Dickens has used language to create contrast.

In pairs, then as a class, discuss why Dickens has included two such sharply contrasting settings in the novel. What is he trying to show the reader? Write a paragraph to explain the contrast between the two settings and what Dickens was trying to convey. Refer to the wider social context in which the novel is set. Use quotations to support your ideas.

Whole text responses

The puppet sideshow * / **

> **Objectives**
> - to use words, images and sound imaginatively to retell a known story
> - to demonstrate engagement with a text by making it come alive.

Create puppets of the main characters in *Hard Times* and re-tell the story. Resource 6.19 (*Scene cards for a puppet show*) provides cards so that the story can be divided between groups. Allow pupils to decide how to stage the puppet show and what puppets would be most appropriate – finger puppets work well and are quick and simple to make. Pupils will need to re-examine character descriptions and settings to ensure accuracy and each scene will need to be scripted. Encourage pupils to bring together all the knowledge they have developed whilst studying the novel. When each scene is ready, perform the whole story to an audience, either of parents or other pupils who have not studied the book. Video the show so that the puppeteers can view their own performances after the event.

The cover design * / **

> **Objective**
> - to reflect a chosen aspect or theme of a novel through the use of image.

In order to design a book cover, pupils will need a clear understanding of the narrative in order to choose a theme. The website http://www.bl.uk/learning/images/dickens/large116572.html contains a set of British Library circus posters from the Victorian era, so this could form the inspiration for a book cover which focuses on circus. Alternatively, pupils might feel that the mill would represent the theme of the novel more effectively, with its social comment on the middle-class exploitation of workers. Using knowledge developed through the *Those dark satanic mills* activity, design and paint a cover which reflects this aspect of the book. Will the image design be just on the front of the cover or will it wrap around? Complete the activity by writing the blurb for the back cover. A set of book review templates to suit a range of ages is also available as resource 2.16 *A Christmas Carol*.

Create a wiki * / **

> **Objectives**
> ● to respond to, and write reflectively about, a text
> ● to acknowledge and constructively discuss other views about the same text.

Using your VLE, create a wiki for *Hard Times*. As your class reads and explores the book, invite pupils to contribute their thoughts about any aspect of what they have read or learnt. This can be directed by a question from you, or pupils' own discussions can emerge as study of the book continues.

This can also be used to post links to other related titles – start by adding the books listed as linked reading at the conclusion of this chapter. Pupils can then comment on these books and add links of their own. If this is consistent with school policy, parents can also contribute their views and thoughts in a parents' area. The great strength of this is the development of a broad view of a text as the study of it develops, as others within the community can also comment. For the teacher it carries the extra advantage of assessment potential, as the wiki can provide evidence of achievement which can be accessed at any time; this is an opportunity for assessment in addition to evidence collected orally through discussion.

Household words ***

> **Objective**
> ● to consider the effect of *Hard Times* on a reader.

Hard Times was initially published as a weekly serial in the newspaper *Household Words*. Write a review of *Hard Times* to be published the week after the last instalment. Write as a Victorian, so do not just review the story; include a moral reaction to the novel. Review Dickens' aims in writing the book. What did he want to say to readers about society, values and industrial development? Did he achieve what he set out to do?

Portfolio ***

Objective

● to build a portfolio of work which uses a range of response media to demonstrate understanding of the themes and characters of a novel.

In the course of the study suggested in *Whole text plan 11–14* (available on the CD), the following responses can be retained to build into a portfolio. This will demonstrate understanding of the themes of the novel and its main characters. It will also show the ability to use a range of media when responding to the study of a novel.

● a PowerPoint presentation of initial research into an aspect of Victorian society
● a LinkedIn profile for Mr Gradgrind
● an advertisement, poster and flyer for the media campaign, propagating the views of either Mr Gradgrind or Mr Bounderby
● role on the wall sheets for Mrs Sparsit, Sissy and Louisa
● Twitter feeds for two chosen characters
● scripts and the recording of a Jeremy Kyle scene which includes the characters of Stephen Blackpool, Mr Bounderby, Rachael and Stephen's wife
● photographs from the *Whoosh* of Chapters 14–16 (if *Whole text plan 11–14* is used)
● a copy of the speech from the class debate about trade union membership
● Mr Gradgrind's press release explaining his change of view about education
● a Wanted poster for Stephen Blackpool
● *In Memoriam* movie for Stephen Blackpool
● a recording of *The gossips go to town* drama after Bounderby is revealed as a liar
● a book review article of *Hard Times* for *Household Words*.

◯◯◯ Linked reading

Leon and the Place Between: Graham Baker-Smith and Angela McAllister, Templar.
Mill Girl – A Victorian Girl's Diary 1842–1843: Sue Reid, Scholastic.
Annie: The Story of a Victorian Mill Girl: Margaret Nash, Hodder Wayland.
Avoid Working in a Victorian Mill: John Malam and David Antram, Book House.
You Wouldn't Want to be a Victorian Mill Worker! A Gruelling Job You'd Rather Not Have: John Malam, David Antram and David Salariva, Children's Press.
Victorian Factory: Susie Brooks, Wayland.
Trouble at the Mill, My Side of the Story: Philip Wooderson, Kingfisher.
The Way We Live Now: Anthony Trollope, Oxford Classics.
The Way We Live Now: DVD (2006), David Suchet, Matthew MacFadyen.
North and South: Elizabeth Gaskell, Penguin Classics.
North and South: DVD (2005), Daniela Denby-Ashe, Richard Armitage.
Shirley: Charlotte Bronte, Wordsworth.

Note

1 Bracketed figures represent chapter numbers for editions which have been numbered consecutively.

7 *Oliver Twist*

Overview

Context and social background

Until 1834, there was little organised care for the poor. Parishes could build workhouses and make inhabitants work for their keep or they could distribute money directly to the poor, although this was at the discretion of the parish officers. In 1834, the Poor Law stated that all parishes must build a workhouse to care for dependent people. Whole families had to go into the workhouse if the father was ill, died or was unable to earn enough money to provide for the family. Men, women and children were split up, given uniforms to wear and had their hair cut short. Disease was common and spread quickly. When Dickens put the words 'I want more' into the mouth of Oliver Twist, those words represented to the Victorian social conscience not just more food, but also more clothes, more warmth and more care than was given to workhouse children.

Poor children had to work. Between the ages of five and ten, some boys worked as chimney sweeps. Other children (both boys and girls) worked in brick or match factories or in mills. Accidents were common and many children suffered from diseases related directly to their work. Some children who lived on the streets sold matches, lace, flowers or muffins. Others worked as crossing sweepers. Many street children became beggars, pickpockets and petty thieves in order to survive.

Wealthy Victorian boys were educated at home by a tutor or governess until they were old enough to go to grammar or public schools. Girls received very little education. Poor children received no education at all until ragged schools were started – the first one was opened by John Pounds in Portsmouth in 1818. Children of all ages met in a single room and older children taught the younger ones. In a letter to the *Daily News* in 1852, Charles Dickens wrote after a visit to Field Lane Ragged School that the boys 'were difficult of reduction to anything like attention, obedience, or decent behaviour' and 'UNUTTERABLY IGNORANT'. He blamed the government of the day for ignoring the needs of poor children, to the extent that many very young children were already repeat offenders and hardened criminals – a situation that he described as being 'enough to break the heart and hope of any man'.

When Thomas Barnardo arrived in London in 1866 he was horrified to find so many children living on the streets. The following year, he opened a ragged school in order to give a basic education to many street children. In 1870, Barnardo opened his first orphanage – by the time he died in 1905, there were ninety-six homes. Boys were trained for a trade and girls were trained to go into service. Barnardo even set up a fostering scheme for unmarried mothers, arranging for their child to be fostered near to the home where the mother was in service, so that families could be kept together as much as possible.

For two years of his childhood and a further three teenage years, Charles Dickens lived a few houses away from the Cleveland Street workhouse, which was built in 1775 in the parish of St Paul's, Covent Garden. Dickens would have seen the Beadle walking along the street and the paupers being taken into the workhouse. He may also have seen notices similar to the one posted in *Oliver Twist*, offering a child for £5. Worse still, the blacking factory where he was sent to work when his father was admitted to Marshalsea Debtors Prison was in Covent Garden. Cleveland Street workhouse would have been a perpetual threat and he may have worked with children from the workhouse. The name of the notorious pickpocket Fagin, who was cast as a Jew in the novel, was taken from Bob Fagin, with whom Dickens worked in the factory. It was certainly a period that etched itself so deeply in his consciousness as to affect his writing.

The Jewish population of London was not large until the Russian pogrom of 1881, when the number of Jewish immigrants to England increased significantly. There was some religious prejudice, although some Jews, most notably Disraeli, served in public life and a few were elevated to titles and peerages. In 1833 the first Jew was allowed to become a barrister and Jews were allowed full access to all aspect of public life, including entry to universities and all professions by 1890.

This is Dickens' second novel, which was originally published in instalments in *Bentley's Miscellany* between 1837 and 1839. It was published as a novel by Richard Bentley, the owner of the journal, under the name of Boz. Dickens wrote it to draw attention to the effects of the Poor Law and the living and working conditions of many of London's children.

Synopsis

The book opens with a description of Oliver's birth and early struggle to breathe. His unmarried mother dies just after he is born, so he is handed over to the parish to be cared for. At the age of nine he is moved to a workhouse to be trained for a trade, but falls foul of the authorities when he draws the short straw and asks for more gruel on behalf of all the boys. An attempt to indenture Oliver as a chimney sweep's boy at a cost of £3.50 to the parish fails when the magistrate refuses to sign the papers. He is eventually taken by Mr Sowerberry the undertaker to be apprenticed. He is trained as a mute and becomes very popular with bereaved mothers.

After he is badly treated in the undertaker's house, Oliver runs away, walking seventy miles to London. He meets Jack Dawkins (better known as the Artful Dodger) and is introduced to Fagin. After learning to pick pockets, he is allowed onto the streets. He sees the Artful Dodger picking a pocket for which Oliver himself is arrested and tried. He is only saved when the shop keeper arrives at court to defend him. Mr Brownlow, the victim of the crime, pities Oliver and takes him home.

Whilst nursing him back to health, Mr Brownlow is repeatedly struck by a similarity in Oliver's appearance with a painting of a young lady on his wall. Meanwhile, Fagin, scared that Oliver will inform against him, sends Nancy to find out where he is. When Oliver is trusted to pay a bill and return some books to the bookseller, Nancy kidnaps him and returns him to Fagin.

Oliver is handed over to Bill Sikes and used to break into the Maylies' house at Shepperton. The robbers are disturbed, Oliver is shot and Bill abandons him in a ditch. The following morning, Oliver is found, Dr Losberne is sent for and he is nursed back to health by Mrs Maylie and her adopted niece, Rose. When he regains strength, Oliver is taken to London, only to discover that Mr Brownlow has moved to the West Indies, so he remains with the Maylies for several more months.

Meanwhile, the action moves to the workhouse where Oliver was born. Sally, the nurse who delivered him, confesses to robbing Oliver's mother of something gold, although she dies without revealing what it was. The matron, now Mrs Bumble, finds a pawnbroker's ticket which she redeems for a gold locket containing two strands of hair and a wedding ring. Mr Monks asks to meet her, purchases the locket for 25 sovereigns and destroys it. He then visits Fagin, revealing that he is Oliver's half-brother. Nancy, overhearing the conversation, warns Rose Maylie that Oliver is in danger.

When Oliver spots Mr Brownlow, who has returned to London, Rose decides to go to him for advice. He, together with Dr Losberne, Harry Maylie and Mr Grimwig, form a committee to consider how best to trap Mr Monks and restore Oliver's inheritance. Nancy meets Rose late one night and describes how to find Monks, but unknown to them, Noah Claypole is spying on them. Bill murders Nancy for her betrayal and goes on the run. He dies trying to escape, Fagin is arrested and hanged and Monks confesses fully. Oliver's mother is named as Agnes Flemming and Rose as her sister. Rose and Harry Maylie marry and Mr Brownlow adopts Oliver, moving to the country so that he can continue to live near the Maylies.

Main characters

- Oliver Twist, the protagonist of the novel
- Mr Bumble, the workhouse Beadle
- Mr and Mrs Sowerberry the undertaker and his wife
- Jack Dawkins, the Artful Dodger
- Mr Brownlow, an old gentleman
- Bill Sikes, Fagin's partner
- Nancy, Bill Sikes' girlfriend
- Mr Monks, aka Edward Leeford, Oliver's half-brother
- Mrs Maylie and her adopted niece, Rose, who care for Oliver when he is shot

Minor characters

- A nurse (Sally) and a doctor who were present when Oliver was born
- Mrs Mann, in charge of the orphanage where Oliver was sent as a baby
- Mr Gamfield the chimney sweep
- Noah Claypole, a charity-boy and Charlotte, workers for the undertaker (alias Mr Morris Bolter and Mrs Bolter)
- Charley Bates, friend of the Artful Dodger
- Mrs Bedwin, Mr Brownlow's housekeeper
- Mr Grimwig, a friend of Mr Brownlow
- Mrs Corney, the matron who cared for the elderly workhouse women, later becoming Mrs Bumble
- Dr Losberne, who cares for Oliver when he is shot and remains close to the Maylie family
- Harry Maylie, Mrs Maylie's son

Settings

- An orphanage, known as the farm, for babies and small children
- The workhouse, where orphans were transferred when old enough to work
- An undertaker's shop
- London: Fagin's den
- The streets of London
- A courthouse
- The home of the wealthy Mr Brownlow
- The Maylies' house in Shepperton

Themes

- Child labour and exploitation

- Good versus Evil
- Corruption
- Poverty

Symbolism

- Darkness and fog
- Light

Activities

Hooks, starters and pause points

Story bag * / ** / ***

Dickens describes Oliver as leaving the workhouse with everything he possessed in 'a brown paper parcel, about half a foot square by three inches deep'. Make a similar parcel. In it put a gold locket, a silk handkerchief, a wooden bowl and spoon, a 'brown cloth parish-cap' and some old papers tied into a package with red legal tape.

To develop collaborative discussion skills, put one object on each table in the classroom. Place a group of pupils around each table and ask them to discuss what the object is, what it might be used for and who might own it. Encourage pupils to provide evidence for their view (for example, 'She might be rich because her necklace is made of gold' rather than 'She might be rich') and to challenge each other (for example, 'Why do you think it's a lady?'). Older pupils can record ideas in writing. After five minutes, rotate pupils to the next table and repeat the process. When all the objects have been examined, hold a whole class discussion about who might own them and what has been learnt. List ideas, then read the first part of the story, to the point where Oliver asks for more.

Food, glorious food * / **

Ask pupils how often they feel hungry. When they feel hungry, what do they do? What is their favourite food? Can they imagine what it would be like to be permanently hungry? *Oliver Twist* is probably best known for the musical version, so listen to the song *Food, Glorious Food* from the musical. This was sung by the boys in the workhouse when they were fantasising about food. What different foods can children hear mentioned in the song? Are any of these foods their favourite? If they were writing a song about food, what would they include in their song? If possible, try to learn the song, maybe even replacing a line or two with pupils' suggestions. Many poor Victorian children were permanently hungry. Explain that the book *Oliver Twist* is the story of a boy who was born and lived for some of his life in the workhouse and he knew what it was to feel hungry and not have enough to eat.

A friend is ... * / **

Some years ago, a daily newspaper used to carry *Love is ...* cartoons, with a different definition of love each day. Some were funny and some were poignant. A similar example is the bumper sticker 'A dog is for life, not just for Christmas'. Ask pupils to produce a cartoon entitled *Friendship is ...* with a slogan which shows the humour, meaning or value of friendship. Share these and discuss all the different aspects of friendship that the cartoons and captions highlight.

The reader is told that Oliver has no friends once he leaves the farm, the orphanage where workhouse babies and children were sent until they were old enough to work. Once he was returned to the workhouse, Oliver was alone. As a result, and also because he was sent out to work when he was just ten years old, he lacked the maturity to make good friendship choices. Parts of the novel explore his choices and the consequences. Link this to a discussion with pupils about how friendship choices are made, and what some of the characteristics of a good friend are.

Roll of the dice ***

Each pupil should roll two dice and give a corresponding number of pieces of information. The topic can be anything relevant to the task – information about a character, a particular part of the plot, the social or cultural context of the novel or the content of a particular lesson. It provides an immediate opportunity for assessment as well as allowing pupils to recall and reinforce new learning.

What would Nancy do? ** / ***

This activity helps pupils to focus on an individual character and to use their knowledge to predict how a given character would behave in particular situations. In each of these situations, decide what Mr Brownlow, Fagin, the Artful Dodger and Nancy would do:

- seeing a pickpocket working
- seeing a homeless child crying in the street
- seeing a child being beaten by an adult
- being offered stolen goods
- being asked for money or food by a beggar
- seeing someone drop their wallet.

Discuss the actions that each character would have taken and how their different characters determined their choices. What information about each character did pupils use to make their decision? Focus on Nancy – she would always make the sensitive, kind or sympathetic choice. What does this tell the reader about her?

Understanding character

What's in a name? * / **

> **Objectives**
>
> - to relate the experience of the central character to the experience of the reader
> - to understand how Dickens wrote from a different time and place from the present
> - to interrogate a text to deepen and clarify understanding and response.

Read aloud the section of the story when Oliver is named (text extract 7.1 *What's in a name?*). Does this still happen today? Ask pupils to talk to their families about how and why their first names were chosen and what they mean. Where does their surname come from? How does this demonstrate belonging? Through shared discussion, explore how family influences a sense of identity – for example, do pupils look like a parent or sibling? How do they know they belong to their family? How would children feel if their name had been chosen by a complete stranger?

The text doesn't mention how Oliver felt about his lack of family – perhaps because survival in a workhouse was a higher priority, or perhaps because so many children were orphaned that it was not an unusual experience. Ask children to relate Oliver's experience to their own. What might it feel like not to belong to anyone? List the vocabulary that this discussion generates and retain it.

Ask each child in your class to design a name picture for themselves. For younger children, this could be just their name. For older children, this could include the meaning of their name. Produce a name collage by joining all the designs together. Alternatively, provide each child with a square of plain fabric on which to draw their design using fabric pens. Join the fabric squares together to form a name quilt. Oliver could be given a square in the middle of the quilt or collage, with the children's words written around his name.

Finding a friend * / **

> **Objectives**
> - to relate the experience of the protagonist to the experience of the reader
> - to deduce characters' reasons for behaviour from their actions.

At one point in the narrative, Dickens writes, 'The boy had no friends to care for, or to care for him'. Several people befriend Oliver at key points in the novel. We are told that he cried when he left his first home, the farm where workhouse babies were cared for, because 'he was leaving behind the only friends he had ever known'. On the morning that Oliver ran away from the Sowerberrys, he visited the farm to say goodbye to Dick, his closest friend from his life there. At the end of the novel, Oliver returns to visit him, only to find that he has died. He is then next befriended by Jack Dawkins, the Artful Dodger, and although the Artful Dodger just sees a good opportunity to train Oliver as a pickpocket, Oliver misinterprets this as friendship. After his false arrest and release, he is then befriended by Mr Brownlow. This friendship turns out to be more enduring – Mr Brownlow not only cares for Oliver, he helps to unravel his history and prove his parentage, before finally adopting Oliver and bringing him up as his own son. Nancy also cares for Oliver and even though she kidnaps him from Mr Brownlow to return him to Fagin, she eventually sacrifices her own life to save Oliver.

Read text extract 7.2 (*Finding a friend*) either aloud to pupils or through shared reading. Discuss what each extract in turn tells the reader about the person and how good a friend each one is. Why did Oliver think that the Artful Dodger and Fagin were good friends? At what point did he realise what their real intentions were? How did Mr Brownlow show friendship and what effect did this have on Oliver?

After detailed discussion, divide pupils into groups and provide them with the text extract for one character. Ask them to highlight all key words in the text which describe the character or what the character did for Oliver. Then create a Wordle image, using www.wordle.com. Compare the images for the Artful Dodger and Mr Brownlow. What do the images tell you about their respective characters? Which one was a reliable friend? Experiment with colour and font to enhance this contrast further.

Bill Sikes ** / ***

> **Objective**
> ● to examine how an author makes word choices to create a character type.

Bill Sikes was a housebreaker who used Oliver to break into the house of the Maylies in Shepperton. There is nothing in the book which suggests that Bill had any good in him at all. He was violent, threatening everyone who annoyed him. At the end of the book, he kills Nancy for betraying him in order to save Oliver. He is hunted by the police but dies trying to escape capture. Text extract 7.3 (*Bill Sikes*) describes Bill's appearance and something of his actions. After reading and discussing the extract, design a *Wanted* poster which the Bow Street Runners might have printed after the Maylies' house was broken into (resource 7.1 *Wanted*).

Sleeping with the coffins ***

> **Objective**
> ● to consider a Victorian social issue through Oliver's eyes.

Child labour was part of Victorian society and workhouse children were sent to work from the age of seven. Discuss the work which Oliver has been sold to do and think about how a young child might feel about it. Read text extract 7.4 (*Sleeping with the coffins*), which describes his first night at the undertaker's. What atmosphere has Dickens evoked? How has he used language to do this? What is the paramount emotion that Oliver experiences? What words tell the reader this?

Using the text extract, information from the discussion, film stills or other book images, pupils should create a piece of work reflecting Oliver's state of mind. Pupils can choose the mode of presentation, but truthfulness to the text must be observed, together with the intended outcome of exploring the social issue of child labour through the eyes of a child. Share responses, in each case discussing how emotion is communicated and whether it is effectively portrayed.

Power play ***

> **Objective**
> ● to analyse relationships within the novel.

Read the dialogue scenes between Fagin and Bill Sikes in either Chapter 13 or Chapter 15 closely. Think about their relationship. Discuss who has the power and how this is portrayed in the dialogue. Is there any evidence of the balance of the relationship other than dialogue? Working with a partner, recreate one of these scenes as a performance dialogue. Think about how you can show the power play between the two men. Watch each performance and discuss the decisions that each pair of performers made. Were they effective? Was any of the prose surrounding the dialogue interpreted? Add any informative prose to the discussion. How has Dickens used language to demonstrate the power play between these two characters?

Victim or traitor? ***

Objective

● to explore Dickens' creation of the character of Nancy and consider reasons for her behaviour.

There are several points in the narrative when Nancy showed herself to be caring, particularly about Oliver. She did not want to kidnap Oliver and return him to Fagin and, having done so, became angry with Fagin when he threatened to hit Oliver. What were the reasons for this? At one point in the narrative, Fagin describes Nancy to Monks as 'Only one of my young people'. What does this tell the reader about Nancy's dependence on both Fagin and Bill? Did she want to spare Oliver from the fate that she knew awaited him? Read Chapters 45 to 47, in which Noah spies on Nancy and overhears her telling someone about Fagin's plot against Oliver. Bill and Fagin interpret her actions as betrayal and Bill murders her in a fit of rage. But Rose Maylie interpreted Nancy's behaviour very differently and understood that Nancy was putting herself in danger to help Oliver. So, was Nancy a victim of her circumstances desperately trying to save Oliver, or a double crosser who deserved what happened to her?

After group discussion, pupils should prepare a speech supporting one of these two views of Nancy, using evidence from Chapters 45 to 47, together with any other evidence which is recalled from earlier in the story. Hold a class debate and conclude by holding a ping-pong debate – on one side of the classroom stand all the people who agreed that Nancy was a victim and on the other side, all those who thought that she was double crossing Bill and Fagin. The first pupil makes a point and someone on the opposite side steps up and rebuts the comment with an opposing statement. At the conclusion of the activity, have a show of hands to determine the majority view. Remind pupils that points must be supported by evidence or quotations and that challenges can be made during the debate if points are not adequately supported.

Why did Dickens include the character of Nancy in *Oliver Twist*? What is her role in the plot, particularly in relation to Oliver? What does the character tell the reader about the criminal underclass of Victorian society, its view of women and the possibilities of social mobility for girls like Nancy?

Understanding plot

What's for tea? * / **

Objectives

● to relate the experience of the central character to the experience of the reader
● to understand how Dickens wrote from a different time and place from the present
● to use drama strategies to explore the issue of hunger
● to empathise with the characters and debate the moral dilemma portrayed in the description of the workhouse food.

Local waterworks provided workhouses with an unlimited supply of water. Local corn merchants provided small quantities of oatmeal and this formed the ingredients of gruel, the staple diet of workhouse inhabitants. Children were given a porringer of gruel (a shallow bowl measuring between ten and fifteen centimetres in diameter) three times a day. Gruel was made by boiling oatmeal in water to make thin porridge. Twice weekly an onion was added and on Sundays, children were given about 65 grams of bread. Dickens describes this in the book, saying that the local Boards 'contracted with the water-works to lay on an unlimited supply of water; and with a corn-factor to supply periodically small quantities of oatmeal; and issued three meals of thin gruel a day, with an onion twice a week, and half a roll on Sundays'. Make some gruel and show children what they would have had to eat if they had lived in a workhouse. Discuss what it would be like to be constantly hungry and compare this with a modern diet. What would the impact have been on the children's health?

Read the text extract 7.5 (*What's for tea*) from Chapter 2 which describes where the boys were fed. Read to the point where Oliver asks for more and Mr Bumble is summoned. Then play word tennis. In pairs, children should re-tell the story, saying one word or phrase each until the story is complete. Then, through shared discussion, list the characters (the master, one or two ladies to assist in dispensing the gruel, the boys and Mr Bumble), the setting (the large stone hall with the copper where the gruel was made and which the boys looked at longingly) and the action (the gruel being ladled, the boys gobbling the food, licking the bowls, spoons and fingers clean, Oliver being nudged and encouraged by the boys into asking for more, being hit over the head with a ladle for asking and Mr Bumble being called).

Dividing children into groups, give each group a different part of the story to freeze frame (resource 7.2 *What's for tea*). Share frames and discuss what each frame communicates and how it might be improved. Take digital images of each freeze frame and using these, ask each group to storyboard the story. Encourage the person taking the digital images to think about camera angles – how could a high angle shot be used in frame one to show the insignificance of the boys? And how could low angle shots in frames five and six demonstrate the power relationship between the adults and children? From the storyboards, produce shadow puppets of the characters and make a shadow puppet film, with children providing dialogue using Dickens' own words where possible. Think about the speed of the dialogue and consider the effect of silence. Complete the activity by sharing all the films. What has been learnt about:

- life for workhouse children
- Oliver's character
- Mr Bumble's character
- how well the Board cared for orphaned children?

Mantle of the expert – life in the workhouse * / **

> **Objectives**
> - to explore a complex issue through working in role
> - to work logically and methodically to test ideas and make deductions
> - to write a formal, non-chronological report, using points which emerge through research.

Mantle of the expert is a drama strategy developed by Dorothy Heathcote to encourage an enquiry-based approach to learning. Pupils are placed in a situation in which they must work in an expert role to investigate or research a particular aspect of the situation. In this mantle of the expert activity, pupils will work in role as Poor Law Commissioners, investigating the state of workhouses with particular reference to children, and reporting back to the government with their findings.

Care for the poor was not a Victorian creation. Laws to determine who was responsible for the poor in each parish came into existence during Tudor times, with Acts of Parliament in 1597 and 1601. Workhouses were increasingly built as provision for the poor in the following centuries. In 1833, with concern being publicly expressed about the conditions of some work-houses, in which disease and malnutrition were common, the Prime Minister, Lord Grey, set up a Poor Law Commission with powers to investigate the country's workhouses. The Commission ran from the passing of the Poor Law in 1834 (which stated that all children should receive three hours of education daily in a workhouse school) until 1847. It was closed after the discovery that the manager of the Andover workhouse in Hampshire was stealing so much that the residents were literally starving.

Resource 7.3 (*Letter from the Prime Minister*) provides a letter from the Prime Minister (who was Lord Melbourne by the time the Commission started its work) inviting pupils to join the Commission. There were three founding Commissioners, Thomas Frankland Lewis, George Nicholls and John George Shaw-Lefevre, who quickly appointed assistants as the task was so big. They were all required to swear an oath of office, so the resource includes an oath that all pupils must swear before taking office. Once taken, this oath empowers them, as Commissioners, to ask any questions they wish, interview anyone they wish and then report their findings to the government. *Commissioners' passes* are provided as resource 7.4.

The PowerPoint as resource 7.5 (*Workhouse children*) provides access to a range of work-house materials, which Commissioners can interrogate for facts. They can also make their own decisions about other suitable sites to visit or records to read in the form of books. They should then compile a report to deliver – a sample text is available as resource 7.6 (*Workhouse Commissioners' Report exemplar*) for modelling formal report writing with pupils before they embark on their own reports (resource 7.7).

A day in my life ** / ***

Objectives
- to understand how a writer from a different time uses the plot of a novel to portray experiences
- to demonstrate empathy with a character through writing in role.

Children in the workhouse were expected to work from the age of nine. Sometimes they worked locally and sometimes they were apprenticed; an option preferred by the Board officials as the child was no longer the responsibility of the parish. Read text extract 7.6 (*A day in my life*), which describes Oliver's apprenticeship to an undertaker. This account is typical of a workhouse child's life in the workplace – he was bullied by other children, fed on scraps which would other-wise have been given to the dog, and left to sleep under the shop counter among the coffins. He was trained to walk in front of funerals as a mute – this was particularly popular for the funer-als of children. His apprenticeship should have lasted for seven years, so he was faced with three choices – carry on, return to the workhouse or run away. Children who chose the latter option then lived on the streets, earning a living as a crossing sweeper (sweeping the roads clear of horse droppings and rubbish before ladies and gentlemen crossed them), selling matches, begging or stealing. Street gangs in London were common.

After reading this section of Oliver's story and discussing his experience, ask pupils to decide on the key events, listing and retaining them. Also list some key words about how Oliver felt. Readers are given no hint about this at the point when he actually ran away, so pupils will need to think in role to choose this vocabulary, bearing in mind that at this point he is in control of his own life, which was neither the case in the workhouse nor when apprenticed to Mr Sowerberry. Then, talking in role, rehearse an account of a day in Oliver's life, before writing a recount for a magazine article entitled *A day in my life*. A text sample (resource 7.8 *A day in my life*) is provided for modelling or shared reading before pupils write independently. This could be followed by pupils writing about a day in their own lives as a contrast.

Loss of innocence ***

> **Objective**
> ● to explore Oliver's continuing loss of innocence.

'Loss of innocence' is a phrase which describes an experience of pain, suffering or trauma which causes a child to grow up quickly. As such, the whole novel could be considered as a narrative of the loss of innocence. Using text extract 7.7 (*The journey to London*), ask pupils to write five or six tweets documenting Oliver's thoughts and feelings during his journey to London, including at least one about his surroundings and one about the people he met. Show how these incidents caused him distress and contrast this with the relief which he must have felt when he was shown kindness. Remember the 140 character limit.

Crossed lines ***

> **Objective**
> ● to understand the structure of a novel.

Crossed lines (resource 7.9) is a resource on which to plot the structure of *Oliver Twist* as the novel is read. Calculate how many different people Oliver has come into contact with at any given point in the story and add Oliver to a crossed lines chart showing his interaction with each group. Add any details to the relevant strand of the chart even if Oliver is not present, if the action is something that affected him. The chart can also be used to predict the outcome of a particular plot strand. Foreshadowing can be noted, together with any unanswered questions.

Lost identity ***

> **Objective**
> ● to make links between the parallel narratives, exploring Oliver's involvement in them.

Read text extract 7.8 (*Lost identity*) and re-read the section of Chapter 1 which relates to Oliver's mother. Can the character of Oliver's mother, Agnes, be filled out from the details of the locket? Through discussion, list all the questions that this scene raises. For example, who is Monks and how does he know about the locket? He was introduced into the narrative through a meeting with Fagin, whom he appeared to know. Why is the locket so significant? Who might Agnes be?

After discussing as many questions as can be raised, attempt to create the character of

Agnes and her back story. Then watch this scene using the ITV interpretation of *Oliver Twist*, which provides a complete back story. How does the film version compare with pupils' versions? Are all the predictions plausible? How might Dickens bring the strands of the narrative together effectively? Predict whether the role of Monks is going to become more significant.

Action! ***

> **Objective**
> - to understand how an author structures writing in order to control the pace of the narrative.

Controlling and manipulating language in order to achieve a required effect is an advanced writing skill. Dickens was a master of the art of controlling the reader through the pace of his writing. Compare the opening three paragraphs of Chapter 50 with the closing three paragraphs of the same chapter. What do you notice about the pace of the narrative? How is this achieved? What is the effect of this on a reader? Discuss sentence structure, sentence length and choice of words.

Then, use this knowledge for a language study. Compare Bill's flight in Chapter 50 with Oliver's journey to London in Chapter 8. How is language used by the author in both cases? How is the narrative paced? What does it tell you about the different paces at which Bill and Oliver are fleeing their respective situations? Why are there these differences? Finally, ask pupils to write two paragraphs, one describing Oliver's flight and one describing Bill's flight in their own words, demonstrating how to pace narrative to control the reader. When complete, pair pupils to read and review their writing and evaluate its effectiveness. End with a discussion about what has been learnt from the language study about Dickens' manipulation of language to achieve a required effect.

Understanding setting

Down your street * / **

> **Objectives**
> - to use language to recreate experiences
> - to visualise and comment on events, characters and ideas in *Oliver Twist*, making imaginative links to personal experiences.

Charles Dickens grew up a few houses away from the Cleveland Street workhouse. As a young child, and then again as a teenager, he would have seen the Beadle walking people into the workhouse, including children being moved from the 'farm' where they were placed as babies and left until the parish decided they were old enough to be moved into the workhouse and start work. Dickens would have seen the undertakers regularly delivering coffins and workhouse inhabitants being taken into the community to work. He may well have seen posters advertising children for sale into apprenticeships, and chimney sweeps and undertakers arriving to collect their apprentices from the workhouse gates.

Read these descriptions in text extract 7.9 (*Down your street*). Through shared discussion, list the different street scenes that Dickens might have seen each day – chimney sweeps, staff from the workhouse, undertakers collecting bodies, people looking for children to work for them, notices being put up outside of the workhouse and goods being moved around on donkeys. What does Mr Bumble wear? What does Oliver wear and what does he carry when he finally leaves the workhouse?

Then ask pupils to map the road where they live, showing who lives in which house. Ask them to draw pictures or write about the different people in their street, what they wear, what they do and how they travel around. In particular, ask them to describe what the children in their street do, how they play, whom they play with and when. Compare their street scenes with what Dickens would have seen as a child. What are the differences? In particular, how different is life for children?

Den of thieves * / **

Objectives

- to explore how a writer uses language to create a rich setting
- to demonstrate understanding through model making.

Fagin is one of the most colourful characters in *Oliver Twist*. He ran a child gang which survived through street crime, mostly theft and pickpocketing. Although at first Oliver was fed and appeared to be cared about, this was offered in order to bring him in to the gang to be trained as a pickpocket himself. When he was returned to Fagin after Nancy kidnapped him from Mr Brownlow, he tried to escape, once the full realisation of Fagin's activities dawned on him. Although this was part of Dickens' comment on the plight of Victorian street children, there are still parentless immigrant children in our country today who survive in a similar way and for whom the gang is the only social group to which they belong.

Explore the setting of Fagin's den by reading text extract 7.10 (*Fagin's den*), either aloud to your class or through shared or guided reading. Read the first three paragraphs and list all the things that are in the house: tall chimney breasts, barred shutters which are screwed shut, mice, spiders, a fire, rough sacking beds, colourful silk handkerchiefs hanging on a clothes horse, etc. There is a lot of detail to listen to or read in these paragraphs. Once as much detail as possible has been listed, read the final paragraph. What more does the reader learn about Fagin?

Using a shoe box, create a model of Fagin's den, including all of the items listed through shared reading. When the models are complete, compare them with Dickens' original text – how accurate is the detail? These models are actually miniature film sets, so this activity could be further extended by using paragraph three to create a one-minute film using stop frame animation. To do this, take a series of single frame images using a digital camera. If they have no prior experience of film making, pupils will need to experiment with the tiny movements that characters make in order for the film to flow smoothly. When the images are complete, use Media Player to combine the still images into a film. A soundtrack can be added if pupils wish to script the scene as well.

View the films – how close are they to Dickens' original text? What have pupils learnt about the power of Dickens' description in creating effective setting? Which words in the text were the most evocative? How detailed were Dickens' descriptions? What might the implications of this be for screenwriters when adapting *Oliver Twist* for film?

The Victorian underworld ***

> **Objective**
> ● to understand the social setting and context of the novel.

Resource 7.10 (*The Victorian underworld master sheet*) is a quiz about the Victorian underworld in which Fagin and Bill Sykes existed. Using resource 7.11 (*The Victorian underworld grids*) cut up the grids, placing all the questions in one box and all the answers in a separate box. Ask pupils to take one question and one answer. They must then match questions and answers. When all the pairs are complete, provide pupils with resource 7.12 (*The Victorian underworld question sheet*) and share answers so that all pupils can complete the question sheet. Discuss what information from this quiz has created deeper understanding of the organised criminal world into which Oliver was drawn.

People and places ***

> **Objective**
> ● to examine Dickens' use of setting and characterisation and its effect on the reader.

Text extract 7.11 (*People and places*) contains extracts about a number of characters and their settings. Read and analyse the extracts. What do they tell the reader? How has Dickens used language to achieve atmosphere and influence the reader's emotions? Complete a comparison table (resource 7.13 *People and places*) in groups. On completion, one person from each group should move to another group to share and discuss recorded information. Encourage pupils to challenge each other's evidence, particularly where detail has been inferred. Conclude by discussing the effect of language choices on the reader.

Whole text responses

Near and far * / **

> **Objective**
> ● to explore links between the main characters.

Stand a pupil, working in role as Oliver Twist, in the centre of the room. Where would his mother stand? How close should Mr Bumble stand; he was influential in Oliver's life, but is that the same as being close? Where should Mr Brownlow stand in relation to the Artful Dodger? The former was a genuine friend to Oliver, while the latter pretended friendship in order to exploit him.

As an additional activity, provide each character with some lengths of string. They should give one end to Oliver and hold the other end themselves. If they have links with other characters, they should also give them one end of a length of string. So, for example, Fagin would give one end of a piece of string to Oliver and other pieces to Bill Sikes, Nancy and the Artful Dodger. This is a strong visual representation of the web of relationships surrounding the central character of Oliver.

The Jerry Springer show **

Objectives

- to develop drama techniques to explore a given situation in role
- to demonstrate understanding of themes, causes and points of view
- to explore the notion of literary heritage and understand why Dickens' texts are particularly significant.

Working in role, groups should stage a chat show to answer the question 'Should my mother have abandoned me?' This requires collaborative working to review the story of *Oliver Twist*, the characters and their interaction with Oliver, assign roles and stage a filmed show.

But it also requires an empathetic understanding of Victorian moral values, the judgement of unmarried mothers and lack of social services or care structure for unwanted children. It also requires understanding of the social structure of the workhouse and life as a poor Victorian child. When this activity is complete, share the films and discuss what has been learnt about Victorian society. Why are Dickens' novels so important?

Glogster poster * / **

Objective

- to respond to a complete text and demonstrate understanding of its historical and social significance through the creation of a multimedia presentation.

Bring together all of the work on *Oliver Twist* by creating a glogster poster at www.glogster.com. Writing samples, videos and images can all be imported to create an interactive poster and display pupils' work using a contemporary medium.

Dominoes ***

Objective

- to review understanding of character interaction.

Resource 7.18 provides a set of domino cards. A player can only lay a domino tile next to a character with which it has interacted. This interaction must be described as each tile is laid. Blanks can be used as any character which links to Monks or Noah Claypole. The winner is the first player to use all of their tiles, having successfully detailed the interaction of each character that was placed.

Sound track ***

> **Objective**
> ● to consider the effect of the novel on the reader.

Working collaboratively, create a sound track for *Oliver Twist*. This could be a signature song or verse for each character which represents them as a person, or it could be a series of songs or music to represent the key events of the narrative. Discuss sound tracks when they are complete – what different songs has each group chosen? Are they effective? Why are they different?

Oliver's journal ***

> **Objective**
> ● to write in role, creating a piece of extended writing which demonstrates understanding of the themes and issues of a novel from another time.

Write a journal in role as Oliver, tracking all the main events of the novel as they affect Oliver and responding to the issues which each event raises. An entry should be written each time a key event occurs which affects Oliver, either through his direct involvement or because he hears it reported. It is important to track his growth in understanding as events unfold – for example, when he first stays with Fagin, Oliver thinks that the pickpocketing is a game, so it could be described in this way. Record his feelings at the point on the street when realisation suddenly dawned that he was part of a criminal gang.

Oliver's reflections about other characters could also be included, for example what Mr Brownlow might be thinking about Oliver's disappearance and how Oliver would want him to know the truth. Journal entries could include Oliver's feelings about Nancy's kindness, his observations about Bill's treatment of her and his fears for her safety.

Choices, choices ***

> **Objective**
> ● to demonstrate understanding of a text from another time.

In order to complete their study of Oliver Twist, ask pupils to choose from the following options:

● write a synopsis of the story from the perspective of either Fagin, Mr Brownlow or Mr Bumble
● create a five-minute trailer for *Oliver Twist*, deciding on target audience
● write a prequel and sequel for the novel, including details of Agnes' story and how it affected the people around her, and what happened to Oliver after the close of the novel
● work in a group to create a short film for each of the main characters, exploring their personality and showing the reader's reaction to them
● create a modern context in which a novel could be written which would highlight social issues affecting children and young people today. Create a plot outline and sketches of main characters.

⦶⦶⦶ Linked reading

Hettie Feather: Jacqueline Wilson and Nick Sharratt, Doubleday.

Dustbin Baby: Jacqueline Wilson and Nick Sharratt, Corgi.

Too Much Trouble: Tom Avery, Francis Lincoln.

Workhouse: A Victorian Girl's Diary 1871: Pamela Oldfield, Scholastic.

Chimney Child: A Victorian Story: Laurie Sheehan, Anglia Young Books.

Street Child: Berlie Doherty, Harper Collins Children's Books.

The Sweep's Boy (My Story): Jim Eldridge, Scholastic.

Victorian Workhouse (My Story): Pamela Oldfield, Scholastic.

Death of a Chimney Sweep: Cora Harrison, Piccadilly.

Stonecold: Robert Swindells, Puffin.

The Real Oliver Twist: Robert Blincoe – A Life That Illuminates an Age: John Waller, Icon Books.

Fly by Night: Frances Hardinge, Macmillan.

The Bride's Farewell: Meg Rostoff, Puffin.

Resources

Websites about Dickens and his work

- http://www.tes.co.uk/teaching-resource/Charles-Dickens-6047662/is a three-minute video clip of Michael Rosen visiting Dickens' home in Doughty Street, London in which he examines some treasures from the archive.
- http://dickens2012.org/ This website has been set up as an online portal for anyone who wants to celebrate as part of an online community. It will develop during 2012.
- http://www.bbc.co.uk/drama/bleakhouse/animation.shtml is an interactive animation that allows you to select scenes to learn about Dickens' own life.
- http://www.bbc.co.uk/schoolradio/subjects/english/a_christmas_carol Listen to *A Christmas Carol*, in nine episodes.
- http://www.bbc.co.uk/arts/multimedia/dickens/ challenges you to survive Dickens' London, avoiding pickpockets and criminal gangs in your search for Dickens. If you make a bad choice, you will end up in trouble. This is compulsive and really good to help children put Dickens' stories in the context of Victorian London.
- http://www.dickensfellowship.org/ The website of the Dickens Fellowship, which includes details of local representatives around the world.

Websites about Victorian life

- http://www.schoolsliaison.org.uk/lostluggage/train.htm Learn about Victorian life by finding the owner of lost luggage.
- http://www.geffrye-museum.org.uk/learning/walk-through-a-victorian-house/walk-through/ Walk through a Victorian house, examining objects in your search for a missing dog.
- http://www.show.me.uk/hosted/networks/networks.swf Understand more about Victorian transport systems and the effect on trade by moving products by rail, water or road.
- http://www.bbc.co.uk/victorianchristmas/history.shtml Full of detailed information about the history of Christmas Victorian style – food, presents, cards, traditions, carols and games to play.
- http://www.bbc.co.uk/schools/primaryhistory/victorian_britain/ Explore life as a Victorian child at school, at work and at play. This is a fully interactive website, full of learning potential.
- http://www.woodlands-junior.kent.sch.uk/Homework/victorians/children/ Investigate what life was like for Victorian children through using images supported with simple text.
- http://www.nettlesworth.durham.sch.uk/time/victorian/vindex.htm Lots of information about the lives of Victorian children. The section on child labour and the Industrial Revolution provides useful research material for examining the jobs which children did and a contrast between city and country.

General interest

- http://www.sfs.org.uk/ The site of the Storytelling Society, with a comprehensive list of story-tellers around the country.
- http://dickensmuseum.com/vtour/index.php Tour each room of Dickens' home in Doughty Street, London.
- http://www.dickensmuseum.com/ for information about news and upcoming events.
- http://www.digitaldickens.com contains a number of brief videos of the buildings which inspired Dickens' settings.
- http://www.charlesdickensbirthplace.co.uk/ A virtual guide of Dickens' birthplace.
- http://www.visitmedway.org/site/attractions/dickens-world-p197391 A tour around the world of Dickens, including the sounds and smells of Victorian street life, a 4D cinema show and an animatronic stage show.
- http://www.pbs.org/wnet/dickens/life_critic.html# A short video clip showing rations which were given in the workhouse.

Booklist

Suitability: To read aloud 7–8 / Independent reading 8–9

- *Oliver Twist and Other Great Dickens Stories*, Marcia Williams, Walker Books: ISBN 9781406305630
- *Illustrated Stories from Dickens*, Usborne Illustrated Classics: ISBN 9781409508670
- *A Christmas Carol*, adapted by J. Collins, illustrated by Chris Russell, Ladybird Children's Classics: ISBN 9780721407456
- *A Christmas Carol* with audio CD, adapted by Lesley Simms, illustrated by A. Marks, Usborne Young Reading: ISBN 9780746058572
- *Bleak House*, adapted by Mary Sebag-Montefiore, illustrated by Barry Ablett, Usborne Young Reading: ISBN 9780746097021
- *David Copperfield*, adapted by Mary Sebag-Montefiore, illustrated by Barry Ablett, Usborne Young Reading ISBN 9780746085639
- *Great Expectations*, adapted by Lesley Sims, illustrated by Barry Ablett, Usborne Young Reading: ISBN 9780746085547
- *Oliver Twist* with audio CD, adapted by Mary Sebag-Montefiore, illustrated by Barry Ablett, Usborne Young Reading: ISBN 9781409505389
  Guided reading pack also available.

Suitability: To read aloud 7–9 / Independent reading 9–11

- *Oliver Twist*, illustrated by Iassen Ghiuselev, Walker: ISBN 9781844280681
- *Oliver Twist*, adapted by Gill Tavner, illustrated by Karen Donnelly, Real Reads: ISBN 9781906230005
- *Great Expectations*, adapted by Gill Tavner, illustrated by Karen Donnelly, Real Reads: ISBN 9781906230012
- *A Christmas Carol*, adapted by Gill Tavner, illustrated by Karen Donnelly, Real Reads: ISBN 9781906230029
- *Hard Times*, adapted by Gill Tavner, illustrated by Karen Donnelly, Real Reads: ISBN 9781906230050
- *Bleak House*, adapted by Gill Tavner, illustrated by Karen Donnelly, Real Reads: ISBN 9781906230043.

- *David Copperfield*, adapted by Gill Tavner, illustrated by Karen Donnelly, Real Reads: ISBN 9781906230036
- *Quentin Blake's A Christmas Carol*, Pavilion: ISBN 9781843651215

Suitability: Independent reading 11–14

- *A Christmas Carol: The Graphic Novel Original Text*, adapted by Sean Michael Wilson, illustrated by Terry Wiley, Classical Comics: ISBN 9781906332181
- *A Christmas Carol: The Graphic Novel Quick Text*, adapted by Sean Michael Wilson, illustrated by Terry Wiley, Classical Comics: ISBN 9781906332181
- *Great Expectations*, adapted by James Riordan, illustrated by Victor Ambrus, OUP: ISBN 9780192741905

Suitability: Adult and older readers

Full texts can be found at

- *A Christmas Carol* http://www.dickens-literature.com/A_Christmas_Carol/index.html
- *Bleak House* http://www.dickens-literature.com/Bleak_House/index.html
- *David Copperfield* http://www.dickens-literature.com/David_Copperfield/index.html
- *Great Expectations* http://www.dickens-literature.com/Great_Expectations/index.html
- *Hard Times* http://www.dickens-literature.com/Hard_Times/index.html
- *Oliver Twist* http://www.dickens-literature.com/Oliver_Twist/index.html

General background

- *Charles Dickens: Scenes from an Extraordinary Life*, Mick Manning and Brita Granstrom, Frances Lincoln Children's Books: ISBN 978 1847801876
- *Charles Dickens: A Life of Storytelling, A Legacy of Change*, Templar: ISBN 9781848771178
- *What's so Special about Dickens*, Michael Rosen, Walker Books: ISBN 9781406302035
- *Charles Dickens: Oliver Twist and Other Tales That Will Make you Ask for More*, Valerie Wilding, illustrated by Michael Tickner, Scholastic: ISBN 9781407131641
- *Charles Dickens: A Very Peculiar History*, Fiona Macdonald, Book House: ISBN 9781908177155
- *Vile Victorians (Horrible Histories)*, Terry Deary, illustrated by Martin Brown, Scholastic: ISBN 9780439944045
- *Villainous Victorians (Horrible Histories)*, Terry Deary, illustrated by Martin Brown, Scholastic: ISBN 9781407104317
- *100 facts on Victorian Britain*, Steve Parker, Camilla de la Bedoyere, Rupert Matthews and Jeremy Smith, Miles Kelly Publishing Ltd: ISBN 9781842369845
- *The Timetraveller's Guide to Victorian London*, Natasha Narayan, Watling St Ltd: ISBN 9781904153115
- *Tales for Hard Times: A Story about Charles Dickens* (Creative Minds Biography Series), David R. Collins, illustrated by David Mataya, Lerner PBS Publishing Group: ISBN 9780822569923
- *You Wouldn't Want to be a Victorian Schoolchild: Lessons You'd Rather Not Learn*, John Malam, illustrated by David Antram, Wayland: ISBN 9780750236010
- *History Spies: The Great Exhibition Mission*, Jo Foster, illustrated by Scoular Anderson, Macmillan Children's Books: ISBN 9780330449014

Films

- *A Christmas Carol* (1951) Alastair Sim, Sir Michael Hordern, George Cole
- *A Christmas Carol* (1999) (PG) Patrick Stewart, Hugh E. Grant
- *A Christmas Carol* (2007) (PG) Kelsey Grammer
- *A Christmas Carol* (2009) (PG) Jim Carrey
- *Bleak House* (2005) (PG) Gillian Anderson, Patrick Kennedy, Denis Lawson
- *David Copperfield* (1974) (PG) David Yelland, Arthur Lowe, Martin Jarvis, Patricia Routledge
- *David Copperfield* (1999) (PG) Emilia Fox, Pauline Quirk, Simon Curtis
- *Great Expectations* (2000) (U) Michael York, Sarah Miles
- *Hard Times* (1977) (PG) Timothy West, Patrick Allen
- *Oliver Twist* (2006) (PG) Ben Kingsley, Jamie Foreman
- *Oliver Twist* (2006) (PG) Robert Lindsay, Keira Knightley
- *Oliver Twist* (2007) (12) Timothy Spall, Rob Bryden

Glossary

alliteration: repetition of a sound at the beginning of two or more words in a phrase or sentence

anaphora: repetition of words at the beginning of several successive sentences or clauses

artistic licence: changing facts in order to make a narrative or film more attractive

atmosphere: the emotional nature of a book or a scene in the narrative

autobiography: a book or story about a person, written by the person themselves

Bildungsroman: literally this means a growth and development novel, a genre in which the protagonist matures in the course of the narrative, often finding answers to significant questions and becoming socially successful.

biography: a book or story about a person's life

caricature: the description of a character in which certain features are unrealistically exaggerated

characterisation: the creation of characters for a narrative

cineliteracy: the ability to evaluate or analyse moving image

connotation: a commonly held cultural or emotional association with the meaning of a word

denotation: the literal meaning of a word

dialogic talk: talk which engages all participants equally

didactic: writing which is intended to instruct the reader

emotive language: an author's deliberate use of words or phrases to evoke a particular emotion in the reader

empathy: recognition of, and identification with, another person's feelings

expanded noun phrase: a group of words formed from two adjectives and a noun

exploratory talk: talk in which participants question each other to explicate thinking and clarify meaning

falling tension: the action of a scene or plotline after it has climaxed

figurative language: a collective term for simile and metaphor

foreshadowing: an author's inclusion of hints in the narrative of events that occur later in the novel

formative assessment: reflective assessment by either teacher or pupil

genre: the definition of a class or type of literature

hyperbole: exaggeration for the purpose of emphasis

metaphor: the use of a word which has a connotation with the item which it is used alongside, without making a direct comparison

mise-en-scène: the design of a set or scene in film

multimodal: narrative which communicates in more than one mode, for example words and sound

onomatopoeia: a word which sounds like the object or item which it is describing

parody: a humorous or ironic imitation of a character for emphasis

pathetic fallacy: ascribing human emotions to inanimate objects

personification: giving life to an inanimate object

plot: the action or the events of a story and the way these are arranged to produce a particular effect in the reader

rhetoric: the use of language for persuasive purposes

rising tension: the action of a scene or plotline as it builds to its climax

semiotic system: modes of communication, such as speech, gesture or sound

setting: the geographical place, social context or historical time in which a story is set. The term can apply to a single scene or an overall text.

simile: a direct comparison of two things, usually using the words 'like' or 'as'

stream of consciousness: an uninterrupted flow of thoughts and emotions by a character in a narrative

summative assessment: formal assessment such as marked work or a test

symbolism: the use of an object to represent something with deeper meaning

tone: the reflection of the attitudes of characters to the reader in a story

unreliable narrator: the narrator of a book or film whose narration is compromised by youth, inexperience or bias

visual grammar: the language used to define image

VLE – virtual learning environment: an area of a network on which teaching and learning materials are shared across the community

Web 2.0 technologies: internet tools that require collaborative contribution, for example, social networking sites

Bibliography

Abrams, M.H. (2005) *A Glossary of Literary Terms*, Boston: Thomson Wadsworth.

Ackroyd P. (1990) *Dickens*, London: Sinclair-Stevenson Ltd.

Ackroyd, P. (2011) *London Under*, London: Chatto and Windus.

Alexander, R. (2008) *Towards Dialogic Teaching: Rethinking Classroom Talk*, Cambridge: Dialogos.

Assael, B. (2005) *The Circus and Victorian Society*, Charlottesville, USA: University of Virginia Press.

Bazalgette, C. (ed.) 2010 *Teaching Media in Primary Schools*, London: Sage.

Bearne, E. and Wolstencraft, H. (2007) *Visual Approaches to Teaching Writing: Multimodal Literacy 5–11*, London: Sage.

BFI Education *Look Again!* http://www.bfi.org.uk/education/teaching/lookagain.

Corbett, P. (2005) *Jumpstart! Literacy Games and Activities for ages 7–14*, London: David Fulton.

Cremin, I., McDonald, R., Goff, E. and Blakemore, L. (2009) *Jumpstart! Drama*, London: David Fulton.

Cunningham, H. (2006) *The Invention of Childhood*, London: BBC Books.

DfES (2006) *Primary National Strategy*, Norwich: HMSO.

Dickens, C. (1966) *Dickens' London*, London: The Folio Society.

Dickens, C. (1995) *Stand Up, Mr Dickens*, illus. Jill Bennett, London: Orion.

Dickens, C. (2003) *A Christmas Carol and other Christmas Writings*, London: Penguin Classics.

Dickens, C. (2003) *Bleak House*, London: Penguin Classics.

Dickens, C. (2003) *Hard Times*, London: Penguin Classics.

Dickens, C. (2003) *Oliver Twist*, London: Penguin Classics.

Dickens, C. (2004) *David Copperfield*, London: Penguin Classics.

Dickens, C. (2004) *Great Expectations*, London: Penguin Classics.

Dickens, C. (2006) *Sketches by Boz*, London: Penguin Classics.

Evans, J. (2009) *Talking Beyond the Page*, London: Routledge.

Farmer, D. (2009) *101 Drama Games and Activities,* www.lulu.com.

Heathcote, D. and Bolton, G. (1996) *Drama for Learning: Dorothy Heathcote's Mantle of the Expert Approach to Education*, Westport, Connecticut: Greenwood Press.

Kress, G. (2003) *Literacy in the New Media Age*, London: Routledge.

Kress, G. and Leeuwen, T. van (2006*) Reading Images: The Grammar of Visual Design*, London: Routledge.

Pullman, P. (1995) *Northern Lights*, London: Scholastic.

Richardson, W.H. (2010) *Blogs, Wikis, Podcasts and Other Powerful Web Tools for Classrooms*, Thousand Oaks, California: Corwin Press.

Robins, G. (2011) Music and Multimodal Text. *English four to eleven* Number 41, pp 4–7.

Royal Shakespeare Company (2010) *The RSC Shakespeare Toolkit for Teachers*, London: Methuen.

Smiles, S. (2008) *Self Help*, Oxford: OUP.

Theodorou, M. (2009) *Classroom Gems: Games, Ideas and Activities for Primary Drama*, Harlow: Longman.

Williams, M. (2002) *Oliver Twist and Other Great Dickens Stories*, London: Walker Books.

Winston, J. and Tandy, M. (2008) *Beginning Drama 4–11*, London: David Fulton Books.

Wise, S. (2009) *The Blackest Streets: The Life and Death of a Victorian Slum*, London: Vintage.

Websites

http://www.barnardos.org.uk (accessed 25.05.11)

http://www.bbc.co.uk/victorianchristmas/ (accessed 26.05.11)

http://channel4.com/history (accessed 06.08.11)

http://www.dickensfellowship.org/save-cleveland-street-workhouse (accessed 02.06.11)

http://www.digitaldickens.com (accessed 21.05.11)

http://www.infed.org (accessed 17.08.11)

www.justice.gov.uk (accessed 20.07.11)

http://www.laura-cenicola.de/brithist2/brithist/8-1-introduction-into-victorian-morality-what-exactly-was-the-victorian-era.html (accessed 10.08.11)

www.nationalarchives.gov.uk (accessed 10.08.11)

http://www.spartacus.schoolnet.co.uk (accessed 10.08.11)

http://www.victorianlondon.org/education/raggedschools.htm (accessed 20.08.11)

http://www.victorianweb.org (accessed 18.08.11)

Index

Taylor & Francis

eBooks

FOR LIBRARIES

ORDER YOUR
FREE 30 DAY
INSTITUTIONAL
TRIAL TODAY!

Over 23,000 eBook titles in the Humanities, Social Sciences, STM and Law from some of the world's leading imprints.

Choose from a range of subject packages or create your own!

Benefits for **you**

▶ Free MARC records

▶ COUNTER-compliant usage statistics

▶ Flexible purchase and pricing options

Benefits for your **user**

▶ Off-site, anytime access via Athens or referring URL

▶ Print or copy pages or chapters

▶ Full content search

▶ Bookmark, highlight and annotate text

▶ Access to thousands of pages of quality research at the click of a button

For more information, pricing enquiries or to order a free trial, contact your local online sales team.

UK and Rest of World: **online.sales@tandf.co.uk**

US, Canada and Latin America:
e-reference@taylorandfrancis.com

www.ebooksubscriptions.com

ALPSP Award for
BEST eBOOK
PUBLISHER
2009 Finalist
sponsored by

Taylor & Francis eBooks
Taylor & Francis Group

A flexible and dynamic resource for teaching, learning and research.